J新書 18

単語と単語、正しい結びつきで覚える

魔法のコロケーション

英会話表現1000

佐藤　誠司
Seishi Sato

Jリサーチ出版

はじめに

　英語の表現力を高めるためには、さまざまなアプローチがあります。表現力の基礎となるのは文法や単語の知識ですが、実際に英語を使う際にはそれだけではカバーできない要素がたくさんあります。

　その1つが、この本で学習する「コロケーション＝単語と単語の結びつき」です。

　たとえば、英単語集などで「insurance＝保険」と覚えただけでは、次のような日本語を英語に直すのは難しいでしょう。

---

① 私は3000万円の生命保険に入っています。
② 私の家には火災保険をかけてあります。
③ この保険は地震の被害を補償します。

---

　①の日本文の内容を英語で表現しようとすれば、「保険に入っている」という意味の英語表現が必要になってきます。この本で学習するのは、そうした知識です。

　それでは3つの日本文の英訳例を見てみましょう。赤い文字の単語の結びつきに着目してください。

---

① **I have 30 million yen worth of life insurance.** 〈動詞＋名詞〉
② **My house is insured against fire.** 〈動詞＋前置詞〉
③ **This insurance covers earthquake damage.** 〈名詞＋動詞〉

①の「保険に入っている」はhave insuranceという2つの単語の結びつきで表現されています。そのことを知らないままでは、この日本文を英文にすることは非常に困難でしょう。

　つまり、この本の主な目的は、**自分の言いたいことを正しい英語で表現する力を高めるために必要な、単語と単語の結びつきに関する知識のバリエーションを広げる**ことなのです。

　本書の前半では、起きてから寝るまでの日常生活を**20のシーン**に分け、それぞれの場面に関連するいくつかの**キーワード**を示して、その語を含むコロケーションを**まとめて効率的に学習**します。とくに利用価値の高い「動詞＋名詞」と「形容詞/名詞＋名詞」の結びつきを重点的に取り上げています。

　そして後半では、シーンを限らず**会話で非常によく使われる基本動詞**を取り上げ、その中でもとくによく使われる重要な「動詞＋(前置詞/副詞＋)名詞」のコロケーションを、**例文とともに学習**していきます。

　本書の内容を完全にマスターすれば、先ほど例に挙げたようなレベルの内容も、すらすら表現できる英語力を養うのに役立つはずです。コロケーションの知識を増やして、英語の表現力を高めていきましょう。

佐藤誠司

はじめに ·· 2
「コロケーション」の重要性 ······························ 6
コロケーションの「種類」 ································· 8
本書の利用法 ·· 12

Chapter 1
シーン＋キーワードで一気に身につく！
生活重要連語800
コロケーション ·················· 15

Scene 1 ▶朝ゴハン コーヒーは濃いめに！ ························· 16
 key word bread ／ egg ／ coffee ／ breakfast ／その他

Scene 2 ▶身じたく 歯を磨いて髪をとかして…。 ····················· 22
 key word hair ／ mirror ／ makeup ／ tooth ／その他

Scene 3 ▶天気 今日の天気はどうかな？ ························· 28
 key word weather ／ rain ／ umbrella ／その他

Scene 4 ▶通勤・通学 電車に乗り遅れる⁉ ······························ 34
 key word train ／ street ／ bus ／ traffic ／ station

Scene 5 ▶会議 会議ではアイデアが大切！ ······················ 40
 key word conference ／ meeting ／ idea ／ plan ／その他

Scene 6 ▶事務・営業 注文を確認しよう！ ······························ 46
 key word sale ／ office ／ order ／ service

Scene 7 ▶パソコン パソコンを起動して、さぁメール！ ··············· 52
 key word Internet ／ e-mail ／ computer ／ data ／ file ／ software

Scene 8 ▶電話 「伝言を預かる」はなんていう？ ················ 58
 key word phone ／ call ／ message ／その他

Scene 9 ▶学校 通っているのはどの学校？ ······················ 64
 key word school ／ class ／ exam ／その他

Scene 10 ▶買い物 値引きしてもらえませんか ······················ 70
 key word price ／ discount ／ shopping ／その他

Scene 11 ▶家で遊ぶ パーティーを開こう！ ··························· 76
 key word video ／ TV ／ movie ／ party ／その他

Scene 12 ▶外で遊ぶ　海や山で遊ぼう！ ·· 82
　key word　camp ／ fire ／その他
Scene 13 ▶ドライブ　ドライブに連れて行って！ ····························· 88
　key word　car ／ drive ／その他
Scene 14 ▶旅行　切符を買って旅に出よう ·· 94
　key word　ticket ／ tour ／ film ／ seat ／ photo ／その他
Scene 15 ▶健康　健康増進のために運動！ ······································· 100
　key word　sport ／ health ／ exercise ／ smoking ／その他
Scene 16 ▶散歩　犬と一緒に公園へ ·· 106
　key word　walk ／ bicycle ／ pet ／ dog
Scene 17 ▶住宅　家を建てるヨ！ ··· 112
　key word　house ／ apartment ／ window ／ door ／その他
Scene 18 ▶家事　洗濯物を取り込んで！ ·· 118
　key word　room ／ floor ／ laundry ／ garbage ／その他
Scene 19 ▶食事　産地直送ってどう表現？ ······································· 124
　key word　food ／ meat ／ table ／その他
Scene 20 ▶入浴・就寝　お風呂に入ってぐっすり眠ろう ···················· 130
　key word　bath ／ sleep ／ light ／ bed ／その他

Chapter 2
シーンにかかわらず会話で使える！
動詞+名詞の結びつき200
コロケーション
········· 137

have ···· 138	draw ···· 156	pay ······ 168	hold ····· 177
make ···· 142	get ······· 158	play ····· 170	leave ···· 178
take ····· 146	give ······ 160	put ······ 172	run ······ 179
break ···· 150	go ········· 162	blow ····· 174	see ······ 180
catch ···· 152	keep ····· 164	call ······ 175	set ······· 181
do ········ 154	lose ······ 166	change ·· 176	turn ····· 182

INDEX ·· 183

「コロケーション」の重要性

コロケーション(collocation)とは、(P2〜3でも軽く触れましたが)「連語（関係）」、つまり**「単語と単語の慣用的な結びつき」**のことです。

たとえば、「お風呂に入る」はenter a bathではなくtake a bath、「大雨」はbig rainではなくheavy rain。また、「バスに乗る」はget on a busですが、「自転車に乗る」はride a bicycleと言います。このような単語同士の結びつきを知っておくことは、**正しい英語を使うための大切なポイント**です。

そして、コロケーションは、「語法（usage）」と密接な関係があります。次の例で考えてみましょう。

> 日本文：地図をかきましょうか。
>
> ○　Shall I draw a map?
> ×　Shall I write a map?

これを、「write − drawの語法（言葉の使い方や言葉づかいの規則）」という視点から説明すると、「writeは文字を書くときに使い、drawは線で図や絵を描くときに使うので、write a mapとは言わない」ということになります。

しかしこれを、「地図を描く＝draw a map」という**連語**として覚えてしまうという"**近道**"もあります。これが、コロケーション学習の考え方です。

そして、日本人にとってコロケーションの学習が重要な理由は2つあります。

1つは、前の例からもわかるとおり、**日本語からの連想で間違った単語を使いやすいこと**が挙げられます。

もう1つは、学校で習ういわゆる**「熟語（idiom）」には、コロケーションの知識が含まれない**ことが多いということが挙げられます。

そもそも「熟語」とは、本来は「take place（行われる）」のように、単語と単語とが結びつくことによってまったく別の意味になるものを言います。また、学習用の英和辞典では、「look at（～を見る）」や「by car（車で）」のような、主として前置詞を含む表現も、しばしば独立した見出し語として熟語と同等に扱われています。

しかし、heavy rainやride a bicycleのようなコロケーションは、**辞書の見出し語としてはふつう出てきません。** そのため、**意識的に学習する必要がある**のです。

コロケーションの「種類」

コロケーションにはいくつかのパターンがあります。シーン別の学習に入る前に、その代表的なものをざっと見ておきましょう。

①動詞＋名詞（＋前置詞） (→ p.137)

主に「〜を…する」と言いたいときに使う表現です。特に、make tea（お茶をいれる）のような**「基本動詞＋名詞」**の結びつきを、できるだけ多く頭にインプットしておきましょう。

☐ eat soup	スープを飲む	間違えやすい!
☐ enter a university	大学に合格する	間違えやすい!
☐ join a club	クラブに入る	間違えやすい!
☐ tell a lie	うそをつく	よく使う!
☐ tell 〜 the way	〜に道を教える	間違えやすい!
☐ lead a happy life	幸福な生活を送る	間違えやすい!
☐ solve a problem	問題を解く	よく使う!

②動詞＋前置詞／副詞＋名詞

go to school（学校へ行く）のような形です。**動詞と前置詞のつながり**を覚えておけば、go to work（仕事に行く）、go to bed（就寝する）のように表現を広げていくことができます。

☐ arrive at the station	駅に着く	よく使う!
☐ listen to music	音楽を聞く	よく使う!
☐ fall in love (with her)	（彼女に）恋をする	
☐ hunt for a job	職探しをする	
☐ look up a word in a dictionary	単語を辞書でひく	
☐ knock on a door	ドアをノックする	
☐ get on the bus	バスに乗る	

③動詞 ＋ 形容詞 / 副詞 (＋ 前置詞)

get sick（病気になる）のように、**動詞の後ろに形容詞を置く場合**があります。また、go home（帰宅する）のhomeは「家へ」という意味の副詞です。

☐ stay home	家に（こもって）いる	<よく使う！>
☐ draw near	近づく	
☐ step aside	脇へ寄る	
☐ run short of ～	～が不足する	
☐ speak ill of ～	～の悪口を言う	

④名詞 ＋ 動詞

「～が…する」という結びつきは、熟語集などには載っていませんが重要です。たとえば「犬が吠えた」は The dog **barked**. ですが、「ライオンが吠えた」は The lion **roared**. と言います。

☐ The light turned red.	信号が赤になった。	<よく使う！>
☐ The sun has set.	日が沈んだ。	
☐ The lot fell on me.	くじが当たった。	
☐ Your nose is running.	鼻水が出ているよ。	
☐ The volcano erupted.	火山が噴火した。	

⑤動詞 ＋ 前置詞 / 副詞

動詞と前置詞や副詞がまとまって1つの意味を表すものは、熟語集などにもしばしば載っています。look for ～（～を探す）やget up（起床する）などがその例です。

☐ aim at ～	～をねらう
☐ compare A with B	A を B と比較する
☐ search for ～	～を探す
☐ catch up with ～	～に追いつく
☐ go through ～	～を経験する

⑥形容詞 / 名詞 / 分詞 + 名詞

名詞と形容詞（など）の間には、**意味上の「相性」**があります。たとえば「狭い通り」は narrow street、「狭い部屋」は small room です（narrow =「幅が狭い」、small =「面積が狭い」）。こうした間違えやすいものに注意しましょう。

《形容詞＋名詞》
- [ ] capital letter　　　　　　　　大文字　　　　　　　間違えやすい!

《名詞＋名詞》
- [ ] bank account　　　　　　　　銀行口座　　　　　　よく使う!

《過去分詞＋名詞》
- [ ] frozen food　　　　　　　　　冷凍食品　　　　　　よく使う!

《〜ing ＋名詞》
- [ ] fishing rod　　　　　　　　　釣り竿

⑦形容詞 / 分詞 + 前置詞

形容詞や分詞の後ろには、**どんな前置詞でも置けるわけではありません**。たとえば kind（親切な）の後ろに置く前置詞はふつう to で、She was **kind to** me.（彼女は私に対して親切だった）のように言います。

- [ ] be interested in 〜　　　　　〜に興味がある　　　よく使う!
- [ ] be based on 〜　　　　　　　〜に基づく
- [ ] be busy with 〜　　　　　　　〜で忙しい

⑧名詞 + 前置詞

数はそれほど多くありませんが、**名詞と前置詞の慣用的な結びつき**にも注意しましょう。たとえば「成功のカギ［秘訣］」は a key to success と言います。

- [ ] a house for rent　　　　　　　貸家
- [ ] a right to a patent　　　　　　特許権
- [ ] room for improvement　　　　改善の余地

⑨ 前置詞＋名詞（＋前置詞）

「**前置詞＋名詞**」は、文の中で**副詞や形容詞の働き**をします。たとえば I'm **in good health**. は「私は健康です」、The bus came **on time**. は「バスは時間通りに来た」の意味です。

- ☐ in charge of ～　　　　～を担当している
- ☐ out of fashion　　　　流行遅れだ
- ☐ on time　　　　　　　時間通りに
- ☐ on fire　　　　　　　燃えている
- ☐ on good terms with ～　～とは親しい間柄だ

⑩ その他

名詞を中心とするさまざまな連語があります。たとえば日本語の「**衣食住**」に当たる英語は food, shelter and clothing です。rain or shine（晴雨を問わず）のような対句もよく使います。

- ☐ way of life　　　　　　生活様式　　　*よく使う！*
- ☐ supply and demand　　需要と供給
- ☐ a cake of soap　　　　1個の石けん
- ☐ state of affairs　　　　事態
- ☐ help wanted　　　　　人員募集〈広告などで使う〉

⑪ 固有名詞

固有名詞は、**最初の文字を大文字で書きます**。Mt. Fuji（富士山）、UN = the United Nations（国連）のような略語も重要。the Olympics（オリンピック）、Tokyo Station（東京駅）など、**theの有無**にも注意。

- ☐ Academy Award　　　アカデミー賞
- ☐ Nobel Prize　　　　　ノーベル賞
- ☐ the Pacific Ocean　　太平洋
- ☐ Tokyo's 23 wards　　　東京23区
- ☐ World Heritage (site)　世界遺産

本書の利用法

Chapter 1
シーン＋キーワードで一気に身につく！
生活重要連語800
コロケーション

日常生活のシーンごとに、よく使う単語＝キーワードを数語ピックアップ。その単語と組み合わせて使われるコロケーションを、効率的にまとめて覚えていきましょう。

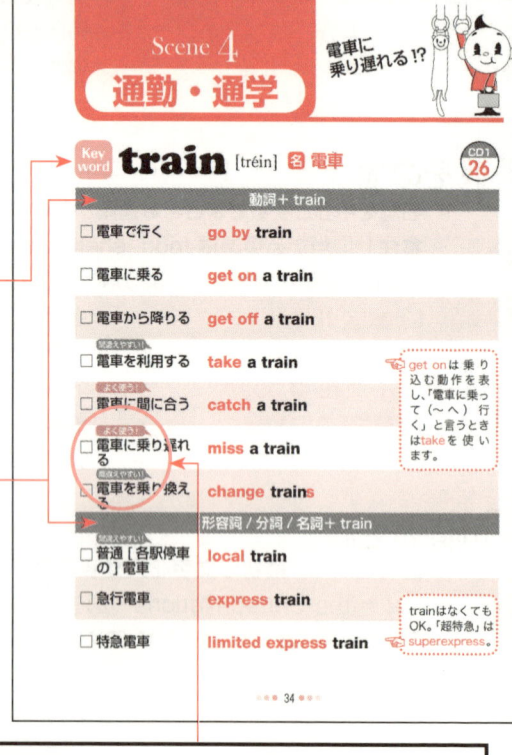

それぞれのシーンには、数語のキーワードが設定されています。

これから学習するコロケーションが、どんなタイプのコロケーションなのかがわかります。
（コロケーションの「種類」については、8ページで解説しています）

よく使う！
英会話でとくに使用頻度が高いものです。

間違えやすい！
日本人がつい間違えやすい表現です。

キーワードを含むコロケーション。生活に密着したものばかりです。赤シートとCD音声（日本語→英語）を活用して、しっかり学習しましょう。

＋αの情報です。使用のヒントや言い換え表現、注意点など、すぐに役立つものばかりなので、ぜひ参考にしてください。

「よく使う！」「間違えやすい！」のコロケーションを中心に、会話フレーズの例文を作りました。CDを聴いて何度も音読し、コロケーションのイメージを刷り込みましょう。

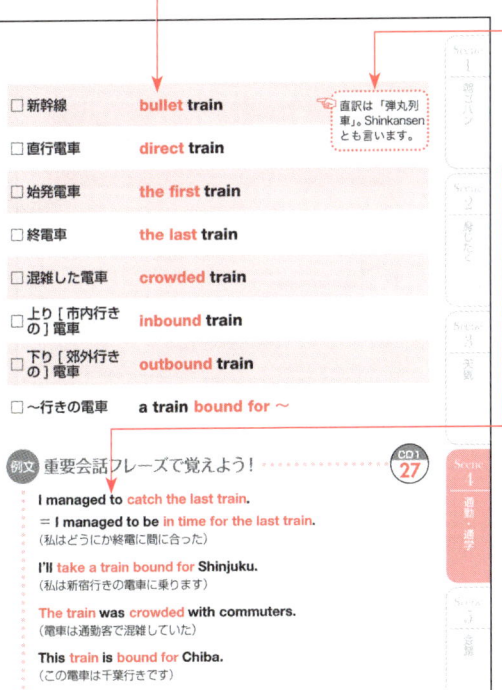

□ 新幹線	bullet train	直訳は「弾丸列車」。Shinkansenとも言います。
□ 直行電車	direct train	
□ 始発電車	the first train	
□ 終電車	the last train	
□ 混雑した電車	crowded train	
□ 上り[市内行きの]電車	inbound train	
□ 下り[郊外行きの]電車	outbound train	
□ 〜行きの電車	a train bound for 〜	

例文 重要会話フレーズで覚えよう！ CD1 27

I managed to catch the last train.
= I managed to be in time for the last train.
（私はどうにか終電に間に合った）

I'll take a train bound for Shinjuku.
（私は新宿行きの電車に乗ります）

The train was crowded with commuters.
（電車は通勤客で混雑していた）

This train is bound for Chiba.
（この電車は千葉行きです）

◆付属CDの内容◆
Chapter 1：見出し語コロケーション（日本語→英語）と「重要会話フレーズで覚えよう！」の会話例文（英語）を収録。
Chapter 2：見出し語コロケーション（英語→日本語）と例文（英語）を収録。

◆赤シートについて◆
付属の赤シートを当てると、コロケーション（の一部）＝赤字部分が消えます。学習の成果を確認する際に利用してください。

Chapter 2
シーンにかかわらず会話で使える!
動詞+名詞の結びつき200
コロケーション

コロケーションのうち、「動詞+名詞」は非常に重要です。ここでは、会話で非常によく使われる24の基本動詞を使った会話頻出コロケーションを学習します。

カギとなる動詞とその基本的な意味を確認。

動詞にプラスされる(前置詞/副詞+)名詞に注目しながら、赤シートとCD音声(英語→日本語)を活用して、しっかり学習しましょう。

Chapter2はすべての見出し語に会話例文がついています。その場面を想像しながらCD(英語音声のみ)を使って何度も音読練習し、イメージをしっかりつかみましょう。

使用する際の注意点や言い換え表現、反対の意味を持つ表現など、すぐに役立つ解説です。

CD2 66
make + 名詞
makeの基本的な意味は「作る」ですが、名詞と結びついてさまざまな表現を作ります。

☐ **make an impression on ~** 〜(人)に印象[感銘]を与える

例文 The film made a deep impression on me.
(その映画は私に深い印象を与えた)

☐ **make a difference** 差が出る;重要である
* make no difference は「差が出ない;どちらでもよい」。

例文 It will make a difference if he helps me.
(彼が手伝ってくれれば差が出るだろう)

よく使う!
☐ **make a living** 生計を立てる
* make は earn でもOK。

例文 She makes a living as a freelance writer.
(彼女はフリーライターとして生計を立てている)

間違えやすい!
☐ **make friends (with ~)** (〜と)仲良くなる
* friend は複数形にします。make a friend などと間違えないように注意。

例文 I made friends with my new classmates.
(私は新しいクラスメイトと仲良くなりました)

... 142

よく使う!
英会話でとくに使用頻度が高いものです。

間違えやすい!
日本人がつい間違えやすい表現です。

Chapter 1

シーン＋キーワードで一気に身につく！
生活重要連語
800
コロケーション

この章ではまず、日常生活を20のシーンに分け、そこでよく使われる「キーワード」を数語設定しました。そして、それぞれのキーワードを含む複数のコロケーションを、種類ごとに表示してあります。コロケーションはどれも、会話でよく使われるものばかりで、種類としては「動詞＋名詞」「形容詞/分詞＋名詞」「名詞＋名詞」が中心です。
例文も活用して、言葉の持つイメージを頭の中に定着させていきましょう！

Scene 1
朝ゴハン

コーヒーは濃いめに！

Keyword **bread** [bréd] 名 パン

 CD1-1

動詞＋bread		
□ パンを焼く	bake bread	bakerは「パンを焼く人＝パン屋さん」。その店がbakery。
□ パンをトーストする	toast bread	
□ パンにバターを塗る	butter bread	breadやtoastは数えられない名詞（物質名詞）なので、a bread [toast]とは言いません。「2枚のトースト」はtwo slices of toast。
□ 食パンを薄切りにする	slice a loaf of bread	
形容詞／名詞＋bread		
□ 1枚のパン	a slice of bread	
□ 自家製のパン	homemade bread	homemade carは「国産車」。
□ やわらかいパン	soft bread	「堅いパン」はhard bread。
□ 焼きたてのパン	fresh bread	「焼きたてのパン」は(a loaf of) bread hot from the ovenとも言います。
□ 古く［堅く］なったパン	stale bread	
□ かびの生えたパン	moldy bread	

Key word egg [ég] 名 卵

動詞＋ egg	
□ 卵を割る	break an egg
□ 卵をかきまぜる	beat eggs

形容詞 / 分詞 / 名詞＋ egg	
□ 生卵	raw egg
□ ゆで卵 よく使う！	boiled egg
□ 目玉焼き よく使う！	fried egg
□ スクランブルエッグ	scrambled eggs
□ ハムエッグ	ham and eggs

「半熟卵」はsoft-boiled egg、「固ゆで卵」はhard-boiled egg。

片面だけ焼いたものはsunny-side up、裏返して軽く焼いたものはover easyです。

例文 重要会話フレーズで覚えよう！

I buttered my bread. = I spread butter on my bread.
（パンにバターを塗った）

You can get various kinds of bread hot from the oven.
（そのパン屋ではいろんな種類の焼きたてのパンが買えます）

How would you like your egg, soft-boiled or hard-boiled?
（卵は半熟と固ゆでどちらがお好みですか）

coffee [kɔ́ːfi] 名 コーヒー

動詞 + coffee	
□ コーヒー豆をひく	**grind** coffee (beans)
□ コーヒーを入れる	**make** coffee
□ コーヒーを注ぐ	**pour** coffee
□ コーヒーをかきまぜる	**stir** one's coffee
□ 【よく使う!】1杯のコーヒーを飲む	**have a cup of** coffee
□ コーヒーをこぼす	**spill** one's coffee

形容詞 / 分詞 + coffee	
□ 苦いコーヒー	**bitter** coffee
□ 口当たりのよいコーヒー	**mild** coffee
□ 【間違えやすい!】濃いコーヒー	**strong** coffee
□ 【間違えやすい!】薄いコーヒー	**weak** coffee
□ ブラックコーヒー	**black** coffee
□ ミルク入りのコーヒー	**white** coffee

> コーヒー豆をひく道具は coffee mill。

> brew coffee とも言います。brewは「火にかけて煎じる；醸造する」という意味。breweryはビールなどの醸造所のこと。

> 複数の場合は、have+〈数〉+ cups of coffee です。

> 「濃い」につられてthickと言わないように注意。

> 「薄い」につられてthinと言わないように。また、「アメリカンコーヒー」は和製英語です。

☐ カフェイン抜きのコーヒー	**decaffeinated coffee**	decaf (coffee) とも言います。
☐ 香りのよいコーヒー	**fragrant coffee**	
☐ 昼食の後のコーヒー	**after-lunch coffee**	
☐ 缶コーヒー	**canned coffee**	

coffee ＋名詞

☐ コーヒーブレイク	**coffee break**	
☐ 喫茶店	**coffee shop**	coffee house でもOK。

例文 重要会話フレーズで覚えよう！ CD1 5

She and I take turns brewing coffee.
（彼女と私は交替でコーヒーを入れます）

He is reading a newspaper, stirring his coffee with a spoon.
（彼はコーヒーをスプーンでかきまぜながら新聞を読んでいる）

I spilled my coffee on the floor by mistake.
（私は誤ってコーヒーを床にこぼした）

I have two cups of coffee.
（私は毎日2杯のコーヒーを飲みます）

I'd like my coffee strong.
（コーヒーは濃くしてください）

Let's take a coffee break.
（コーヒーブレイクにしましょう）

Key word: breafast [brékfəst] 名 朝食

動詞 + breakfast

☐ 朝食のしたくをする	**fix** breakfast	
☐ （十分な）朝食をとる	**have** (a good) breakfast	「〜な朝食をとる」はhave a 〜 breakfastと表します。
☐ 朝食をとりそこなう	**miss** breakfast	
☐ 朝食を抜く	**skip** breakfast	

形容詞 / 分詞 + breakfast

☐ 軽い朝食	**light** breakfast	「たっぷりの朝食」はheavy breakfast。
☐ バランスのとれた朝食	**balanced** breakfast	
☐ ヨーロッパ式の朝食	**continental** breakfast	パンとコーヒーだけの軽い朝食のこと。対してイギリス式の朝食（English breakfast）にはベーコンエッグ・マーマレードつきトースト・紅茶などがつきます。

例文 重要会話フレーズで覚えよう！

Skipping breakfast is bad for your health.
（朝食を抜くのは体に悪い）

I **had a** quick [late] **breakfast**.
（私は急いで［遅い］朝食をとった）

You should have a **balanced breakfast** [diet].
（バランスのとれた朝食［食事］をとるべきだ）

Others その他

動詞＋名詞

- 残り物を食べる **have leftovers**
- 湯をわかす **boil water** — 「お湯」はboiled water。
- スープを温める **warm (up) soup** — レンジで温めるときはnuke soupとも言います。
- 音を立ててスープを飲む **slurp one's soup**
- スープを飲む **have soup** — eat soupでもOK。カップスープのときはdrinkも使えます。
- つまようじを使う **use a toothpick** — 「歯をほじる」はpick one's teeth。

形容詞＋名詞

- こってりしたスープ **rich soup** — 「あっさりしたスープ」はplain [light] soup。
- 乳製品 **dairy product**

例文 重要会話フレーズで覚えよう！

I had leftovers for breakfast.
（朝食に残り物を食べた）

Don't slurp your soup.
（音を立ててスープを飲んではいけません）

Scene 2
身じたく

歯を磨いて髪をとかして…。

Key word **hair** [héər] 名 髪

動詞＋hair

□ 髪にブラシをかける	brush one's hair	「くしでとかす」は comb one's hair。
□ 髪をシャンプーする	shampoo one's hair	
□ 髪を乾かす	dry one's hair	
□ 髪を切ってもらう（よく使う！）	have one's hair cut	have [get] a haircut とも言います。
□ 髪をセットする	set one's hair	
□ 髪を分ける	part one's hair	「髪を七三に分ける」は part one's hair on the side。
□ 髪を結う	do (up) one's hair	
□ 髪を（後ろで）束ねている	wear one's hair tied (at the back)	「髪をお下げ[三つ編み]にしている」は wear one's hair in braids。
□ 髪を染める	dye one's hair	
□ 髪を伸ばしている	wear one's hair long	

形容詞 / 分詞 + hair		
□ 薄い髪	thin hair	
□ 硬い髪	stiff hair	「かつら」は wigとも言います。部分かつらはhairpiece、男性（はげ隠し）用のかつらはtoupeeです。
□ かつら	false hair	
□ 脂性の髪	greasy hair	
□ 直毛	straight hair	「パーマ」はpermanent waveから来た言葉。「天然パーマ」はnatural waveと言います。
□ パーマをかけた髪	permed hair	
□ ウェーブのかかった髪	wavy hair	

例文 重要会話フレーズで覚えよう！ CD1 11

My hair is hard to comb.
（私の髪はとかしにくい）

I had a haircut at the barber's.
（理髪店で髪を切ってもらった）

I'd like my hair parted in the middle.
（髪を真ん中で分けてください）

He has his hair dyed brown.
（彼は髪を茶色に染めている）

My hair is getting thin.
（髪が薄くなってきた）

Key word: mirror [mírər] 名 鏡

動詞 + mirror

□ 鏡に向かう	**face** a mirror
□ 鏡を見る 〈よく使う!〉	**look in** a mirror
□ 鏡に映っている	**be reflected in** a mirror
□ 鏡〈の角度〉を調節する	**adjust** a mirror

mirror + 動詞

□ 鏡が割れた。	The mirror **broke**.
□ 鏡にひびが入った。	The mirror **cracked**.
□ 鏡が曇った。	The mirror **fogged (up)**.

形容詞 / 分詞 / 名詞 + mirror

□ 手鏡	**hand** mirror
□ 姿見	**full-length** mirror
□ 三面鏡	**three-sided** mirror
□ 曇った鏡	**clouded** mirror

☞ triple mirrorでもOK。

Key word: **makeup** [méikʌp] 名 化粧

動詞 + makeup

- 化粧する（よく使う！） **do** one's makeup
  → **put on** one's makeupとも言います。
- 化粧をしている（よく使う！） **wear** makeup
- 化粧を直す **fix** one's makeup
  → **touch up** one's makeupとも言います。
- 化粧をやり直す **redo** one's makeup
- 化粧を落とす **remove** one's makeup
  → **take off** one's makeupでもOK。

形容詞 + makeup

- 厚化粧（よく使う！） **heavy** makeup
  → **thick** makeupでもOK。「薄化粧」は**light** makeup。
- 最小限の化粧 **minimal** makeup

例文 重要会話フレーズで覚えよう！

The mirror is clouded from the steam.
（鏡が湯気で曇っている）

I'm not **wearing makeup** now.
（今は化粧をしていません）

She always wears **heavy makeup**.
（彼女はいつも厚化粧をしている）

Key word **tooth** [túːθ] 名 歯（複数形は teeth）

動詞＋ tooth

□ 歯を磨く（よく使う！）	brush one's teeth	「歯ブラシ」は toothbrush、「練り歯みがき」は toothpaste。
□ 歯を直す	fix a tooth	
□ 悪い歯を抜く	pull out a bad tooth	
□ 歯が抜ける	lose a tooth	

形容詞 / 分詞 / 名詞＋ tooth

□ 虫歯	decayed tooth	cavity とも言います。
□ 前歯	front tooth	
□ 奥歯	back tooth	
□ 永久歯	permanent tooth	「乳歯」は baby tooth。
□ 親知らず	wisdom tooth	
□ 義歯；入れ歯	false tooth	denture とも言います。
□ 歯並びが悪い	have crooked teeth	

Others その他

動詞＋名詞

- 歯医者へ行く　**go to the dentist('s)**　☞「歯医者さんにみてもらう」は see a dentist。
- うがい薬でうがいをする　**gargle with mouthwash**
- トイレを借りる　**use a bathroom**　☞ borrowは「借りて持って行く」という意味なので使えません。
- トイレの水を流す　**flush a toilet**

形容詞＋名詞

- 公衆トイレ　**public lavatory**

例文 重要会話フレーズで覚えよう！

I brush my teeth after every meal.
（私は毎食後に歯を磨きます）

I need to have my teeth fixed.
（歯を直してもらわなくちゃ）

I had a bad tooth pulled out at the dentist's.
（歯医者で悪い歯を抜いてもらいました）

The toilet won't flush.
（トイレの水が流れない）

May I use the bathroom?
（トイレをお借りできますか）

Scene 3
天気

今日の天気はどうかな？

Key word: **weather** [wéðər] 名 天気

形容詞 / 分詞 / 名詞 ＋ weather

□ 好天	**good** weather	fair weatherでもOK。ちなみにfair weather friendとは「都合のいいときだけ近づいてくる友人」のこと。
□ 悪天候	**bad** weather	
□ ひどい天気	**terrible** weather	
□ 絶好の天気	**perfect** weather	ideal weatherでもOK。
□ はっきりしない天気	**unsettled** weather	
□ 不快な天気	**unpleasant** weather	dull [gloomy] weatherとも言います。
□ じめじめした天候	**damp** weather	
□ 蒸し暑い天候	**sultry** weather	muggy weatherでもOK。hot and humid weatherとも言います。
□ うだるような暑さ	**boiling** weather	
□ 変わりやすい天気	**changeable** weather	

weather ＋動詞	
☐ 天気は回復しそうだ。	**The weather will improve.**
☐ 天候が許せば	**weather permitting**

weather ＋名詞	
☐ 天気予報	**weather forecast** — weather reportでもOK。
☐ 天気予報官	**weather forecaster**
☐ 天気図	**weather map** — weather chartでもOK。
☐ 気象台	**weather station**

例文 重要会話フレーズで覚えよう！ CD1 19

The weather is changeable in autumn.
（秋の天気は変わりやすい）

Weather permifting, we'll go fishing on Sunday
（天候が許せば、私たちは日曜日に釣りに行きます）

Today's weather is ideal for a sports day.
（今日の天気は運動会には絶好だ）

The weather forecast says that it'll be fair, later cloudy.
= According to the weather report, it'll be fair, later cloudy.
（天気予報によれば、晴れのち曇りだ）

Key word rain [réin] 名 雨 動 雨が降る

動詞＋rain

- 雨が降りそうだ。 **It looks like rain.**
- 雨が降り出した。 **It began raining.** → rainingはto rainでもOK。
- 雨がやんだ。 **It stopped raining.**
- 雨宿りをする **take shelter from the rain**

形容詞 / 分詞＋rain

- 霧雨 **fine rain** → fineは「細かい」という意味。fine snowは「粉雪」です。
- どしゃ降りの雨 **pouring rain** → torrential rainでもOK。
- 横なぐりの雨 **driving rain**
- 降ったりやんだりの雨 **intermittent rain** → 「にわか雨」はshower、「夕立」はevening shower。
- 大雨 **heavy rain**

例文 重要会話フレーズで覚えよう！

We had a **heavy rain** last night.
(ゆうべ大雨が降りました)

I **took shelter from the rain** under a tree.
(木の下で雨宿りをした)

Key word: **umbrella** [ʌmbrélə] 名 傘

動詞 + umbrella

- □ 傘をさす　　　　　open one's umbrella
- □ 傘をたたむ　　　　fold one's umbrella

☞ 「傘を上に持ち上げる」は put up [raise] one's umbrella。

- □ 傘を置き忘れる　　leave one's umbrella (behind)
- □ 傘に入れてもらう　share ~'s umbrella

分詞 + umbrella

- □ 折りたたみ傘　　　folding umbrella
- □ 自動開閉式の傘　　self-opening umbrella

umbrella + 名詞

- □ 傘立て　　　　　　umbrella stand
- □ 傘の骨　　　　　　umbrella rib

例文　重要会話フレーズで覚えよう！

Can I share your umbrella?
(傘に入れてもらえますか)

I left my umbrella on the train.
(列車の中に傘を置き忘れた)

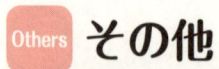 **その他**

名詞＋動詞

□ 雷が光った。	Lightning flashed.	
□ 雷が鳴った。	Thunder rolled.	Thunder cracked.でもOK。
□ 木に雷が落ちた。	The tree was struck by lightning.	
□ 虹が出た。	A rainbow appeared.	
□ 強風が吹いている。	The wind is blowing hard.	「向かい風」は head wind、「追い風」は tail [following] wind。
□ 風がやんだ。	The wind has died down.	
□ 雪が解けてなくなった。	The snow has melted away.	

形容詞／名詞＋名詞

□ 梅雨	the rainy season	
□ 寒冷前線	cold front	「梅雨前線」は rain(y) front。
□ 寒波	cold wave	「熱波」はheat wave。
□ 暖冬	mild winter	mild climateは「温暖な気候」。
□ 残暑	the heat of late summer	

☐ 真夏日	**tropical day**
☐ 空模様	**the look of the sky**
☐ 降水確率	**precipitation percentage**
☐ 強風注意報	**storm warning**
☐ 摂氏10度	**10 degrees centigrade** ～ degrees CelsiusでもOK。
☐ 零下10度	**10 degrees below zero**

例文 重要会話フレーズで覚えよう！

The rainy season has set in.
(梅雨に入った)

The rainy season is over.
(梅雨が明けた)

A cold wave hit the Kanto region.
(寒波が関東地方を襲った)

Judging from the look of the sky, it'll begin to rain.
(空模様から判断すると、雨になりそうだ)

A storm warning is in force for Tokyo.
(東京に強風注意報が出ている)

The temperature is 32 degrees centigrade.
(気温は摂氏32度だ)

Scene 4
通勤・通学

電車に乗り遅れる!?

Key word **train** [tréin] 名 電車

動詞＋ train	
□ 電車で行く	go by train
□ 電車に乗る	get on a train
□ 電車から降りる	get off a train
□ 電車を利用する 〔間違えやすい!〕	take a train
□ 電車に間に合う 〔よく使う!〕	catch a train
□ 電車に乗り遅れる 〔よく使う!〕	miss a train
□ 電車を乗り換える 〔間違えやすい!〕	change trains

> get onは乗り込む動作を表し、「電車に乗って(〜へ)行く」と言うときはtakeを使います。

形容詞 / 分詞 / 名詞＋ train	
□ 普通 [各駅停車の] 電車 〔間違えやすい!〕	local train
□ 急行電車	express train
□ 特急電車	limited express train

> trainはなくてもOK。「超特急」はsuperexpress。

□ 新幹線	**bullet** train	☞ 直訳は「弾丸列車」。Shinkansenとも言います。
□ 直行電車	**direct** train	
□ 始発電車	**the first** train	
□ 終電車	**the last** train	
□ 混雑した電車	**crowded** train	
□ 上り[市内行きの]電車	**inbound** train	
□ 下り[郊外行きの]電車	**outbound** train	
□ ～行きの電車	a train **bound for** ～	

 例文 重要会話フレーズで覚えよう！ CD1 27

I managed to catch the last train.
= I managed to be in time for the last train.
（私はどうにか終電に間に合った）

I'll take a train bound for Shinjuku.
（私は新宿行きの電車に乗ります）

The train was crowded with commuters.
（電車は通勤客で混雑していた）

This train is bound for Chiba.
（この電車は千葉行きです）

street [stríːt] 名 通り

動詞＋ street

□ 通りをふさぐ	**block** a street
□ 通りを閉鎖する	**close** a street
□ 通りを横切る	**cross** a street
□ 通りに面する	**face** a street

☞ crossingは「交差点；横断歩道」。

形容詞＋ street

□ 裏通り	**back** street
□ 交通[往来]の激しい通り 〔間違えやすい！〕	**busy** street
□ 行き止まりの通り	**dead-end** street
□ 人影のない通り	**empty** street
□ 活気のある通り	**lively** street
□ 狭い通り	**narrow** street
□ 本通り	**main** street

☞ 「激しい交通」は heavy traffic。

☞ 「寂しい通り」は lonely street。

☞ 「広い通り」は wide street。

Key word: **bus** [bʌ́s] 名 バス

CD1 29

形容詞 / 名詞 + bus

☐ 通勤・通学のバス **commuter** bus

☞ 「バスで通勤する」はcommute by bus。

☐ シャトルバス **shuttle** bus

☐ 長距離バス **long-distance** bus

bus + 名詞

☐ バスの便 bus **service**

☐ バス停 bus **stop**

☐ バスターミナル bus **depot**

例文 重要会話フレーズで覚えよう！

CD1 30

The street is blocked with snow.
(その通りは雪で通れない)

He crossed the street against the red light.
(彼は赤信号を無視して通りを横切った)

My office faces the main street.
(私のオフィスは本通りに面しています)

There is no bus service to the village.
(その村へはバスの便がありません)

How can I get to the bus stop?
(バス停へはどう行けばいいですか)

Key word: **traffic** [trǽfik] 名 交通

動詞 + traffic		
□ 交通を規制する	**restrict** (the) **traffic**	
□ 交通を妨げる	**block** (the) **traffic**	interrupt (the) trafficでもOK。
□ 交通を停止させる	**back up** (the) **traffic**	tie (the) trafficでもOK。

形容詞 + traffic		
□ 激しい交通 (間違えやすい!)	**heavy traffic**	muchやmanyは使えません。「少ない交通」はlight traffic。
□ 一方通行	**one-way traffic**	

traffic + 名詞		
□ 信号機	**traffic signal**	
□ 交通渋滞 (よく使う!)	**traffic jam**	trafficはcongestionでもOK。
□ 交通規制	**traffic regulation**	
□ 交通違反	**traffic offense**	「スピード違反」はspeeding、「スピード違反の摘発装置」はspeed trap。
□ 交通違反切符	**traffic ticket**	警官が交通違反者に渡すカード。

Key word: **station** [stéiʃən] 名 駅

station ＋名詞

□ 駅員	**station attendant**	「駅長」は station-master、「車掌」は conductor。

形容詞 / 名詞＋ station

□ 最寄り駅 (よく使う!)	**nearest station**	
□ 間違った駅	**wrong station**	
□ 乗り換え駅	**transfer station**	transferは「乗り換え切符」という意味でも使います。
□ 地下鉄の駅	**subway station**	
□ 終着駅	**terminal station**	

例文 重要会話フレーズで覚えよう！

I was caught in a traffic jam on my way to work.
（出勤の途中で交通渋滞に巻き込まれた）

Traffic is restricted because of the festival.
（祭りのために交通が規制されている）

The accident backed up traffic for 10 kilometers.
（その事故で10キロにわたって交通が渋滞した）

Can you tell me the way to the nearest station?
（最寄りの駅へ行く道を教えてもらえますか）

I got off at the wrong station.
（降りる駅を間違えた）

Scene 1 朝ゴハン
Scene 2 身じたく
Scene 3 天気
Scene 4 通勤・通学
Scene 5 会議

Scene 5 会議

会議ではアイデアが大切!

Key word: **conference** [kάnfərəns] 名 会議

※「会議」を意味する語には、meeting、conference、council、session、convention などがあります。

動詞 + conference

会議の段取りをする	**arrange** a conference
会議を召集する	**call** a conference

☞「議長」は chairperson や president や moderator など。

形容詞 / 名詞 + conference

緊急の会議	**emergency** conference
学会	**academic** conference
記者会見	**press** conference
テレビ会議（間違えやすい！）	**video** conference

☞「報道発表」は press release。

☞ TV conference とは言いません。

conference + 名詞

会議室	conference **room**
会議の出席者	conference **attendee**
会議の議題	conference **agenda**

Key word: **meeting** [míːtiŋ] 名 会議　CD1-35

動詞＋meeting

□ 会議を開く（よく使う!）	**hold** a meeting	「開かれる」は be held。take place（行われる）も使えます。
□ 会議をさぼる	**skip** a meeting	
□ 会議を延期する	**postpone** a meeting	put off a meetingでもOK。
□ 会議を中止する	**cancel** a meeting	call off a meetingでもOK。
□ 会議に出席する（よく使う!）	**attend** a meeting	「出席者」は attendant。「会議に欠席する」は be absent from a meeting。
□ 会議を中座する	**leave** a meeting	
□ 会議の司会をする	**chair** a meeting	

形容詞／名詞＋meeting

□ 定例会議	**regular** meeting	
□ 週1回の会議	**weekly** meeting	
□ 年次総会	**annual** meeting	
□ 総会	**general** meeting	「役員[理事]会」は board of directors とも言います。
□ 役員会	**board** meeting	

Scene 1 朝ゴハン
Scene 2 身じたく
Scene 3 天気
Scene 4 通勤・通学
Scene 5 会議

☐ 予算会議	**budget** meeting	
☐ 担当者会議	**staff** meeting	
☐ 販売促進会議	**sales** meeting	
☐ 昼食をとりながらの会議	**lunch** meeting	

☞ 「販売[営業]部長」はsales manager。

例文 重要会話フレーズで覚えよう！ CD1-36

The video conference lasted for hours.
（テレビ会議は何時間も続いた）

The conference was arranged for May 10th.
（会議は5月10日に決まった）

The receptionist took me to the conference room.
（受付係は私を会議室へ案内してくれた）

The sales meeting will be held next Friday.
（販売促進会議は来週金曜日に開かれます）

The meeting was postponed till next month.
（会議は来月まで延期されました）

He sometimes skips meetings and goes to the coffee shop.
（彼は時々会議をさぼって喫茶店へ行く）

I have to leave the meeting in the middle.
（私は会議を途中で抜けねばなりません）

Who will chair the meeting next week?
（来週の会議は誰が司会をしますか）

Key word: **idea** [aidíːə] 名 考え

動詞＋idea

□ アイデアを思いつく **よく使う!**	hit on an idea	come up with an ideaとも言います。come to ～（～の頭に浮かぶ）という言い方も覚えておきましょう。
□ わかる	get an idea	
□ まったくわからない［知らない］ **よく使う!**	have no idea	
□ 案を実行に移す	put an idea into practice	

形容詞／名詞＋idea

□ 名案	good idea	「非現実的な考え」はimpractical idea。practical jokeは「悪ふざけ」
□ 現実的な考え	practical idea	
□ 持論	pet idea	

例文 重要会話フレーズで覚えよう！

I **hit on** a good **idea**.
= I **came up with** a good **idea**.
= A good **idea came to** me.
（いいアイデアを思い付いた）

Your **idea** is difficult to **put into practice**.
（君の案を実行に移すのは難しい）

Keyword: **plan** [plǽn] 名 計画；案

CD1-39

動詞 + plan

日本語	英語	備考
□ 計画を立てる **よく使う!**	**make** a plan	**draw up** a plan でもOK。
□ 提案する	**suggest** a plan	**propose** a plan でもOK。「提案」は **suggestion** または **proposal**。
□ 案を採用する	**adopt** a plan	
□ 案を断念する	**give up** a plan	
□ 計画を実行する **よく使う!**	**carry out** a plan	

形容詞 + plan

日本語	英語	備考
□ 具体案	**concrete** plan	**concrete** の反意語は **abstract**（抽象的な）。
□ 試案	**tentative** plan	
□ 弾力的な案	**flexible** plan	
□ 費用効率の高い案	**cost-effective** plan	
□ 時期尚早な案	**premature** plan	
□ 非現実的な案	**unrealistic** plan	

Others その他

動詞＋名詞

- 採決を行う　　　　take a vote
- 多数票を得る　　　get a majority vote
- 提案に賛成の票を入れる　　vote for a proposal
- 提案を棚上げする　　put a proposal on the shelf

> 「提案に反対の票を入れる」は vote against a proposal。

形容詞＋名詞

- 満場一致の票　　unanimous vote

> unanimousの発音は「ユーナニマス」。

例文 重要会話フレーズで覚えよう！

It may be easy to make a plan, but it isn't always easy to carry it out.
（案を立てるのは簡単かもしれないが、それを実行するのは常に簡単とは限らない）

We've decided to adopt his plan.
（私たちは彼の案を採用することに決めました）

Why don't we take a vote on it?
（多数決で決めよう）

The motion was adopted by a unanimous vote.
（その動議は満場一致で採択された）

Scene 6 事務・営業

注文を確認しよう！

Key word: **sale** [séil] 名 販売；売れ行き

CD1 42

動詞＋sale

□ セールをする	have a sale	make a saleでもOK。
□ 売り上げを増す	increase sales	
□ 〜を販売する	put 〜 on sale	
□ 発売される	go on sale	
□ 〜の売り上げに達する	reach a sale of 〜	

形容詞 / 名詞＋sale

□ 訪問販売	door-to-door sales	「通信販売」はmail-order business。
□ 総売上高	gross sales	「純売上高」はnet sales。
□ 在庫一掃セール	clearance sale	saleはなくてもOK。
□ 特売	special sale	bargain saleでもOK。

sale(s) ＋名詞		
よく使う! 販売促進	**sales promotion**	sales drive とも言います。
販売キャンペーン	**sales campaign**	
間違えやすい! 営業マン	**sales representative**	略してsales rep とも言います。representativeは「会社を代表して応対する人」ということ。salesmanやsaleswomanとも言います。
営業部	**the Sales Department**	
売上額	**sales figures**	
売上税	**sales tax**	

例文 重要会話フレーズで覚えよう！ CD1 43

We're having a sale this weekend.
(この週末にセールを行います)

When will the game be put on sale?
(そのゲームはいつ販売されますか)

The book has reached a sale of a million copies.
(その本の売り上げは100万部に達した)

He was promoted to manager of the Sales Department.
(彼は営業部長に昇進した)

Our sales figures have been declining recently.
(最近当社の売上額は落ちている)

Keyword: **office** [ɔ́ːfis] 名 事務所；職場

CD1 44

動詞 + office

☐ 出社する	**go to** the office	タイムカードを押して退社することをpunch [clock] outと言います。出社時に打刻するのはpunch [clock] inです。
☐ 退社する	**leave** the office	
☐ オフィスを開く	**open** the office	
☐ 事務所を移転する	**relocate** the office	

形容詞 / 分詞 / 名詞 + office

☐ 市役所 〔よく使う！〕	**municipal** office	city officeでもOK。city hallとも言います。
☐ 県庁	**prefectural** office	
☐ 本社[本部；本店]	**head** office	
☐ 支社[支店]	**branch** office	officeはなくてもOK。
☐ 貸事務所	**rental** office	
☐ 法律事務所	**law** office	
☐ 秘書室	**secretary's** office	
☐ 設備の整ったオフィス	**well-equipped** office	「～(の設備)を備えている」はbe equipped with ～。

よく使う!		
□ 案内所	information office	

| □ 切符売り場 | ticket office |

| □ 〈学校の〉保健室 | nurse's office |

office ＋名詞

間違えやすい!		
□ 会社員	office worker	

| □ 勤務時間；営業時間 | office hours |

| □ 会社の日常業務 | office routine |

よく使う!		
□ 事務用品	office supplies	

> white-collar workerとも言います。「サラリーマン」も「OL」も和製英語です。英米では「私はサラリーマンです (I'm an office worker.)」のような言い方はあまりせず、具体的な仕事内容で自己紹介するのが普通です。

例文 重要会話フレーズで覚えよう！　CD1 45

I left the office early.
（会社を早退しました）

We've relocated our office to Yokohama.
（当社は横浜に事務所を移転しました）

I work at a law office.
（私は法律事務所に勤めています）

She was transferred to a branch office.
（彼女は支店に転勤になりました）

Our office hours start at 9 a.m..
（当社の営業は9時から始まります）

Key word: **order** [ɔ́:rdər] 名 注文

CD1 46

動詞＋order

□ 発注する **よく使う!**	**place** an order	
□ 受注する	**receive** an order	receiveは「受ける」だけで、応じるとは限りません。「注文を受け入れる」はaccept an orderです。
□ 再発注する	**repeat** an order	
□ 注文を取り消す **よく使う!**	**cancel** an order	revoke an orderでもOK。
□ 注文を確認する **よく使う!**	**confirm** an order	「注文を再確認する」はreconfirm an order。
□ 注文を更新する	**renew** an order	
□ 注文品を配達する	**deliver** an order	「配達」はdelivery。

形容詞＋order

□ 追加注文	**additional** order	
□ 予約注文	**advance** order	advance him $50（彼に50ドルの手付金を払う）のように動詞としても使います。

order＋名詞

□ 注文伝票	**order sheet**

Key word: **service** [sə́ːrvis] 名 サービス

Scene 6 事務・営業

形容詞 / 名詞 ＋ service

☐ **よく使う!** よいサービス　　**good** service　　☞「悪いサービス」は poor service。

☐ 特別サービス　　**extra** service

☐ **間違えやすい!** アフターサービス　　**after-sales** service　　☞「アフターサービス」は和製英語です。

☐ 顧客サービス係　　**customer** service

例文 重要会話フレーズで覚えよう！

I'm calling to confirm our order.
（注文を確認するためにお電話しています）

We can't accept further orders at present.
（当面これ以上の注文は受けられません）

I've already placed an additional order.
（すでに追加注文をしています）

Take this order sheet to the Accounting Section.
（この注文伝票を会計課へ持って行きなさい）

The shop gives good service to their customers.
（その店は顧客によいサービスを提供する）

The computer shop provides good after-sale service.
（そのパソコンショップはアフターサービスがよい）

Scene 7 パソコン

パソコンを起動して、さぁメール！

Key word: **Internet** [íntərnət] 名 インターネット

動詞 ＋ Internet

□ パソコンをインターネットに接続する	connect a computer to the Internet	
□ インターネットにアクセスする よく使う！	access the Internet	
□ インターネットを閲覧する	browse the Internet	browse in a bookstore（本屋で立ち読みする）のようにも言います。
□ ネットサーフィンをする	surf the Internet	

Internet ＋ 名詞

□ インターネットサイト	Internet site	websiteとも言います。
□ インターネット広告	Internet ad	
□ ネットオークション	Internet auction	「入札」はbidding。make the highest bidは「いちばん高い値をつける→落札する」という意味です。
□ インターネット利用者	Internet user	
□ インターネット検索	Internet search	
□ インターネット取引	Internet transaction	

Key word: e-mail [íːméil] 名 e メール

動詞 + e-mail

□ メールを送る (よく使う!)	send an e-mail	
□ メールを受け取る	receive an e-mail	
□ メールを転送する	forward an e-mail	

e-mail + 名詞

□ メールマガジン	e-mail newsletter	☞ e-mail magazineでもOK。
□ メールアドレス	e-mail address	

例文 重要会話フレーズで覚えよう！

I surfed the Internet to learn more about the topic.
（その話題についてもっと知るためにネットサーフィンした）

Keep in mind the danger of Internet transactions.
（インターネット取引の危険を頭に入れておきなさい）

The boss told me to forward the e-mail to all the staff.
（上司は私にそのメールを全職員に転送するように言った）

Let me know your e-mail address.
（あなたのメールアドレスを教えてください）

I bought this laptop computer in an Internet auction.
（このラップトップのパソコンはネットオークションで買いました）

Key word: computer [kəmpjúːtər] 名 コンピュータ；パソコン　CD1 52

動詞 + computer

□ **よく使う!** パソコンを起動する	**start up** a computer	☞ boot (up) a computerとも言います。
□ **よく使う!** パソコンを停止させる	**shut down** a computer	
□ パソコンを再起動する	**restart** a computer	
□ パソコンを操作する	**operate** a computer	
□ パソコンをアップデートする［最新の状態にする］	**update** a computer	

名詞 + computer

□ **よく使う!** ラップトップ型パソコン	**laptop** computer	☞ computerはなくてもOK。
□ **よく使う!** ノートパソコン	**notebook** computer	
□ デスクトップ型パソコン	**desktop** computer	

computer + 名詞

□ パソコンの画面	**computer screen**	☞「液晶画面」はliquid crystal screen。
□ コンピュータを使いこなす能力	**computer literacy**	
□ **よく使う!** コンピュータウイルス	**computer virus**	

Key word: **data** [déitə] 名 データ

動詞 + data

□ データを集める	gather data	☞ collect data でもOK。
□ データを調べる	check data	
□ データを分析する	analyze data	
□ データを処理する	process data	
□ データを入力する	input data	☞ feed data でもOK。
□ データを印字する	print out data	

例文 重要会話フレーズで覚えよう！

It takes 3 minutes to start up this computer.
(このパソコンは起動するのに3分かかる)

All the computers in this office are regularly updated.
(このオフィスのパソコンはすべて定期的にアップデートされています)

Computer literacy is essential for this job.
(この仕事にはコンピュータの操作能力が不可欠だ)

Input the data into the computer.
(データをパソコンに入力しなさい)

After you check the data, print it out.
(データを照合した後で印字しなさい)

Key word: **file** [fáil] 名 ファイル

動詞＋ file	
ファイルを編集する	**edit** a file
ファイルを上書きする	**write over** a file
ファイルを保存する *よく使う!*	**save** a file
ファイルを消去する *よく使う!*	**delete** a file
ファイルのバックアップをとる	**back up** a file
ファイルを圧縮する	**compress** a file
ファイル名を変える	**rename** a file

☞ erase a fileでもOK。eraserは「消しゴム；黒板ふき」。

形容詞／分詞＋ file	
添付ファイル *よく使う!*	**attached** file
永久保存ファイル	**permanent** file
一時ファイル	**temporary** file
最近使ったファイル	**recently used** file

Key word: **software** [sɔ́ːftwèər] 名 ソフトウェア

動詞 + software

□ パソコンにソフトウェアをインストールする	**install** the software on a computer	install an air-conditioner（エアコンを設置する）のようにも使います。
□ ソフトウェアをアップグレード[更新]する	**upgrade** the software	
□ ソフトウェアをダウンロードする	**download** the software	

名詞 + software

□ アプリケーションソフト	**application(s)** software	softwareは数えられない名詞（集合名詞）なので、a softwareとは言いません。an applicationはOKです。
□ 教育ソフト	**educational** software	

例文 重要会話フレーズで覚えよう！

These files are saved on the hard disk.
（これらのファイルはハードディスクに保存されていますよ）

Don't open the file attached to this e-mail.
（このメールに添付されたファイルを開いてはならない）

I've written over the file by mistake.
（誤ってファイルを上書きしてしまった）

Help me install this software on my computer.
（このソフトを私のパソコンにインストールするのを手伝ってください）

You can download the software on-line.
（そのソフトはオンラインでダウンロードできます）

Scene 8
電話

「伝言を預かる」はなんていう？

Key word: **phone** [fóun] 名 電話

※phoneはtelephoneの短縮形です。

動詞 + phone

電話に出る（間違えやすい！）	answer a phone	get a phoneでもOK。
受話器を取り上げる	pick up a phone	phoneはreceiverでもOK。
電話を切る	hang up a phone	a phoneはなくてもOK。
電話を取りつける	install a phone	
君に電話だよ。	You're wanted on the phone.	

phone + 動詞

電話が鳴っている。	The phone is ringing.

形容詞 / 名詞 + phone

携帯電話（よく使う！）	cell phone	単にcellとも言います。また、cellular phone、mobile (phone) とも言います。
有料電話；公衆電話	pay phone	
テレビ電話	video phone	

(tele)phone ＋名詞

- [ ] 電話帳　　　　**phone book**

  > telephone directoryとも言います。

- [ ] 電話ボックス　**phone booth**

- [ ] 電柱　　　　　**telephone pole**

- [ ] 電話料金　　　**telephone rate**

- [ ] 電話交換手　　**telephone operator**

【間違えやすい!】
- [ ] テレフォンサービス **telephone information service**

例文 重要会話フレーズで覚えよう！

Let's keep in contact by cell phone.
(携帯電話で連絡を取り合いましょう)

"The phone is ringing." "I'll get it."
「電話が鳴っているよ」「私が出ます」

I had a phone installed in my apartment.
(アパートに電話を引きました)

I'll look up the address of the office in a phone book.
(その事務所の住所を電話帳で調べます)

I'm calling from a pay phone.
(今公衆電話からかけています)

Key word call [kɔ́:l] 名 通話

動詞＋ call	
☐ 電話をかける **よく使う！**	make a (phone) call
☐ ～に電話をかける	give ～ a call
☐ （～から）電話を受ける	get a call (from ～)
☐ 電話を回す（転送する）	transfer a call
☐ 折り返し電話する	return a call

形容詞 / 分詞 / 名詞＋ call	
☐ 内線電話	internal call
☐ 外線電話	external call
☐ 外からの[外線]電話	incoming call
☐ 外へかける電話	outgoing call
☐ 市内電話 **間違えやすい！**	local call
☐ 長距離電話	long-distance call
☐ コレクトコール	collect call

☞ 「内線」は extension。(Could I have) Extension 5, please?（内線5番をお願いします）のように使います。

☞ 電話を受けた人が料金を支払う通話のこと。

- ☐ 仕事の電話　　**business** call
- ☐ モーニングコール　**wake-up** call 〔間違えやすい!〕

  > 「モーニングコール」は和製英語です。

- ☐ 匿名の電話　　**anonymous** call
- ☐ 緊急電話　　　**emergency** call

  > urgent call でもOK。

- ☐ いたずら電話　**crank** call

例文 重要会話フレーズで覚えよう！　CD1 61

I'd like to make a long-distance call.
（長距離電話をかけたいのですが）

Don't forget to give me a call tonight.
（今晩、忘れずに電話してね）

You got a call from Mr. Imai.
（今井さんから君（の留守中）に電話があったよ）

Let me transfer your call to the Sales Department.
= **I'll put your call through to the Sales Department.**
（お電話を営業部にお回しします）

This is Tanaka Ryo. I'm returning your call.
（田中亮です。お電話をいただいたようで）

I've been getting crank calls.
（いたずら電話がよくかかってくる）

Key word: **message** [mésidʒ] 名 伝言；メッセージ

動詞＋message

伝言を残す **よく使う!**	**leave** a message
伝言を受ける **よく使う!**	**take** a message
伝言を〜に伝える	**give** 〜 a message
伝言をメモする	**write down** a message
伝言を記録する	**record** a message
伝言を調べる	**check for** messages
伝言に目を通す	**read through** a message

Others その他

動詞＋名詞

電話を切らずに待つ	hold the line
受話器を外したままにしておく	leave a receiver off the hook
携帯の電源を切る	switch off one's cell phone

☞ hold on とも言います。「電話を切る」は hang up です。

名詞＋動詞	
電池が切れた。	The battery went dead.
携帯が圏外だ。	My cell phone doesn't work here.

「電話が切れた[通じなくなった]」はThe line went dead.。

形容詞 / 名詞＋名詞	
間違い電話 *よく使う!*	wrong number
フリーダイヤル	toll-free number
市外局番	area code
職業別電話番号簿	yellow pages

tollは「通行料；使用料」という意味です。

例文 重要会話フレーズで覚えよう！ CD1 64

Please leave a message after the beep.
（発信音のあとにメッセージをどうぞ）

I'll give him your message when he comes back.
（彼が戻りましたらご伝言を伝えておきます）

I checked messages on the answering machine.
（留守番電話の伝言を調べました）

I'm afraid you've got the wrong number.
（番号をお間違えではありませんか）

Would you mind switching off your cell phone, please?
（携帯の電源を切っていただけますか）

Scene 9
学校

通っているのはどの学校？

Keyword **school** [skúːl] 名 学校

動詞 + school

よく使う！ ☐ 通学する	go to school	
☐ 学校に通う	attend school	
よく使う！ ☐ 学校を卒業する	graduate from school	
☐ 退学する	leave school	
☐ 停学になる	be suspended from school	
☐ 退学になる	be expelled from school	

「歩いて通学する」はwalk to school、「学校を休む」はbe absent from school。

finish [leave] schoolとも言います。

形容詞 / 名詞 + school

よく使う！ ☐ 小学校	elementary school
よく使う！ ☐ 中学校	junior high school
よく使う！ ☐ 高校	(senior) high school
☐ 専門学校	professional school

primary school とも言います。「幼稚園」はkindergarten。

vocational schoolでもOK。

□ 大学院	graduate school	「大学院生」は postgraduate。
□ 公立学校	public school	「私立学校」は private school。
□ 全寮制の学校	boarding school	
□ 共学校	coeducational school	coed schoolでもOK。「男子[女子]校」は boys' [girls'] school。
□ 姉妹校	sister school	
□ 塾	cram school	prep[preparatory] schoolは「予備校」。
□ 学校に遅刻する よく使う!	be late for school	
□ 学校を休む よく使う!	be absent from school	

school ＋名詞

□ 学校の制服	school uniform	
□ 校則	school rules	
□ 校舎	school building	
□ 修学旅行	school trip	school excursionでもOK。
□ 学園祭	school festival	

Key word class [klǽs] 名 クラス；授業

動詞 + class

☐ 授業に出席する	**attend** a class
☐ 授業を休講にする	**cancel** a class
☐ 授業を休む	**miss** a class
☐ 授業をさぼる	**cut** a class
☐ 授業がある （よく使う！）	**have** a class

> skip a class でもOK。

形容詞 / 分詞 + class

☐ 上級クラス	**advanced** class
☐ 中級クラス	**intermediate** class
☐ 入門クラス	**introductory** class
☐ 2時間目の授業	**the second period** class
☐ 数学の授業	**math** class

> 「初級クラス」は elementary class、「基礎クラス」は basic class。

class + 名詞

☐ クラス会	**class reunion**

例文 重要会話フレーズで覚えよう！

My brother graduated from high school this year.
(弟は今年高校を卒業しました)

Where does your son attend school?
(息子さんはどちらの学校に通っておられますか)

I'm in my second year in junior high school.
(私は中学2年生です)

Our high school is coeducational.
(私たちの高校は共学です)

I was absent from school with a cold.
(風邪で学校を休みました)

My daughter has outgrown her school uniform.
(娘は大きくなって学校の制服が入らなくなった)

The students must observe the school rules.
(生徒は校則を守らねばならない)

We're looking forward to the school festival.
(私たちは学園祭を楽しみにしています)

We went on a school trip to China.
(私たちは中国へ修学旅行に行きました)

The school festival takes place from July 8th to 10th.
(学園祭は7月8〜10日に行われます)

How many classes do you have today?
(今日は何時間授業がありますか)

I'll take the introductory class.
(私は入門クラスに入ります)

We had a class reunion for the first time in 20 years.
(私たちは20年ぶりにクラス会をしました)

Key word: **exam** [igzǽm] 名 試験

※examはexaminationの短縮形です。

動詞 + exam

□ 試験を受ける（よく使う！）	**take** an exam	自分で出願して受ける場合に使います。決められた試験を受ける場合はhave an examと言います。
□ 試験に合格する（よく使う！）	**pass** an exam	
□ 試験に落ちる	**fail (in)** an exam	「赤点を取る」は口語でflunkと言います。
□ 試験でカンニングをする	**cheat on** an exam	

名詞 + exam(ination)

□ 中間試験	**mid-term** exam	「期末試験」はend-of-term [final] exam。
□ 入学試験	**entrance** exam	
□ 司法試験	**bar** exam	

例文 重要会話フレーズで覚えよう！

My son passed the entrance examination.
（息子は入試に合格しました）

We have the mid-term exams next week.
（来週は中間試験だ）

He was caught cheating on the exam.
（彼は試験でカンニングを見つかった）

Others その他

動詞＋名詞

□ 満点を取る	**get perfect grades**
□ 出席をとる	**call the roll**
□ 宿題をする	**do one's homework**

> get 100 percentとも言います。イギリス英語ではget full marksと言います。

形容詞／名詞＋名詞

□ 新学期	**new (school) term**
□ 昼休み	**noon recess**
□ 掃除当番	**cleanup duty**
□ 厳しい先生	**strict teacher**
□ クラブ活動	**club activity**
□ 生徒会	**student council**
□ 卒業式	**graduation ceremony**

> 「寛大な先生」は generous teacher。

> 「入学式」は entrance ceremony。

例文 重要会話フレーズで覚えよう！

The new term begins in April.
（新学期は4月から始まります）

Scene 10 買い物

値引きしてもらえませんか

Key word: **price** [práis] 名 価格；値段

動詞 + price

□ 値引きする	**reduce** the price	cut (down)、mark down、lower なども使えます。
□ 値上げする	**raise** the price	
□ 見積もる	**quote** a price	quote（見積もる）はビジネスでよく使う動詞です。quotation は「見積もり」。

形容詞 / 分詞 / 名詞 + price

□ 安い値段 〔間違えやすい！〕	**low** price	cheap price とは言いません。「高い値段」は high [✗ expensive] price です。
□ 割引価格	**discounted** price	
□ 正価	**net** price	
□ 店頭小売表示価格	**sticker** price	tag price でも OK。
□ 定価	**fixed** price	
□ 手ごろな値段 〔よく使う！〕	**reasonable** price	
□ 手の届く値段	**affordable** price	

□ 特価	**bargain** price	This is a good bargain. (これはお買い得です) のようにも言います。
□ 出血サービス価格	**giveaway** price	
□ 仕入れ値；原価	**cost** price	
□ 小売価格	**retail** price	「卸値」は **wholesale** price。
□ 単価	**unit** price	

price ＋名詞

□ 値札	price **tag**
□ 価格競争；値引き競争	price **war**
□ 値上げ	price **increase**

例文 重要会話フレーズで覚えよう！ CD1 73

I bought this CD at a discounted price.
(このCDは割引価格で買いました)

You can get it at a lower price on the Internet.
(インターネットならより安い値段でそれを買えるよ)

We can't sell it below the cost price.
(原価以下でそれをお売りすることはできません)

This T-shirt doesn't have a price tag (on it).
(このTシャツには値札がついていない)

Key word: **discount** [dískaunt] 名 値引き；割引

動詞 + discount

□ 値切る	**ask for** a discount	「値切る（交渉をする）」は haggle とも言います。
□ 値引きをする	**make** a discount	
□ ～に値引きをする *よく使う!*	**give** ~ a discount	
□ 値引きをしてもらう *よく使う!*	**get** a discount	

形容詞 / 名詞 + discount

□ 現金割引	**cash** discount	（クレジットカードではなく）現金での支払いに対する割引のこと。
□ 特別割引	**special** discount	
□ 従業員割引	**staff** discount	

discount + 名詞

□ 安売り店	**discount shop**	動詞の discount は「割り引く」の意味。

例文 重要会話フレーズで覚えよう！

Could you give me a discount?
（値引きしてもらえませんか）

I got a 10% discount.
（10%の値引きをしてもらいました）

Key word: **shopping** [ʃápiŋ] 名 買い物

動詞 + shopping

よく使う！		
□ 買い物に行く	**go** shopping	go to shop やgo for shoppingとはいいません。
□ 買い物をする	**do** the shopping	

名詞 + shopping

□ オンラインショッピング	**on-line** shopping
□ ウインドーショッピング	**window** shopping

shopping + 名詞

よく使う！		
□ ショッピングモール	shopping **mall**	歩行者専用の商店街を pedestrian mall と言います。
□ 買い物リスト	shopping **list**	
□ 買い物袋	shopping **bag**	
□ ショッピングカート	shopping **cart**	

例文 重要会話フレーズで覚えよう！

I'll go shopping at the supermarket.
（午後スーパーへ買い物に行きます）

I'm doing the shopping for dinner.
（夕食の買い物をしているところです）

Others その他

動詞＋名詞

□ 開業する	**go into business**	go out of business は「廃業」する。
□ お使いに行く	**go on an errand**	run an errand でもOK。
□ 列の後ろに並ぶ	**join the end of a line**	
□ 列に割り込む	**cut into a line**	
□ チラシを配る	**distribute fliers**	
□ 本を万引きする	**shoplift a book**	

形容詞 / 分詞 / 名詞＋名詞

□ デパート〈よく使う!〉	**department store**	departmentは個々の売り場のことで、toy department（おもちゃ売り場）のように言います。
□ 〈スーパーなどの〉レジ	**checkout counter**	「レジ（の機械）」はcash register、「レジ係」はcashier。
□ 商品券	**gift certificate**	
□ ビニール[ポリ]袋〈間違えやすい!〉	**plastic bag**	vinyl（ビニール）は化学の専門用語で、vinyl bag とは言いません。「ポリバケツ」は plastic bucket。
□ 1万円札	**ten-thousand yen bill**	
□ 自動販売機	**vending machine**	

□ 衝動買い	**impulse buying**	buy on impulse は「衝動買いする」。
□ 試供品	**free sample**	free は「無料の」という意味で、free of charge とも言います
□ 卵1パック	**a carton of eggs**	
□ 古書店	**secondhand bookstore**	
□ 免税店	**duty-free shop**	duty-free は「関税（duty）がない」の意味。sugar-free は「無糖の」。
□ お得な買い物	**good bargain**	
□ おつりが足りない。	**The change is short.**	

例文 重要会話フレーズで覚えよう！ CD1 79

Which floor is the furniture department on?
(家具売り場は何階ですか)

There is a long line in front of the checkout counter.
(レジ（のカウンター）の前には長い列ができている)

This pamphlet is free of charge.
(このパンフレットは無料です)

I bought this bag on impulse.
(このバッグを衝動買いしました)

Could you change a ten-thousand yen bill?
(1万円札を両替してもらえますか)

Scene 11 家で遊ぶ

パーティーを開こう！

Key word: **video** [vídiòu] 名 ビデオ

動詞 + video

間違えやすい！ ビデオを借りる	**rent** a video	rentは「有料で借りる」、borrowは「無料で借りる」という意味です。
ビデオの電源を入れる	**plug in** the video	
ビデオの電源を切る	**unplug** the video	
〜をビデオに録画する	**record** 〜 **on** (a) video (tape)	「〜をビデオに撮る」はtake a video of 〜。
〜をビデオで見る	**see** 〜 **on** video	
ビデオを再生する	**(re)play** a video	
ビデオを巻き戻す	**rewind** a video	
ビデオを早送りする	**fast-forward** a video	
ビデオをダビングする	**copy** a video	dub a videoでもOK。
ビデオを消去する	**erase** a video	

形容詞 / 分詞 ＋ video	
□ 宣伝ビデオ	**promotional video**
□ 海賊版ビデオ	**pirate(d) video**
□ 120分のビデオ	**120-minute video**

「数字+ハイフン」の後ろの名詞は単数形。

video ＋名詞	
□ テレビゲーム _{間違えやすい!}	**video game**
□ テレビ電話	**video phone**
□ 動画サイト	**video site**

「テレビ」ですがこの場合TVは使えません。

例文 重要会話フレーズで覚えよう！ CD1-81

I rented this video for 300 yen for a week.
(このビデオは300円で1週間借りました)

My son is always playing video games.
(息子はいつもテレビゲームばかりしている)

I forgot to record the program on a video tape.
(その番組をビデオに録画し忘れた)

I saw the movie on video.
(その映画はビデオで見た)

Rewind the video after you've finished watching it.
(ビデオを見終わったら巻き戻しておきなさい)

Scene 11 家で遊ぶ
Scene 12 外で遊ぶ
Scene 13 ドライブ
Scene 14 旅行
Scene 15 健康

Key word: TV [tíːvíː] 名 テレビ　CD1-82

動詞＋TV

よく使う！ □ テレビを見る	watch TV	「テレビで番組を見る」はwatch a program on TV。
よく使う！ □ テレビをつける	turn on the TV	switch on the TVとも言います。
□ テレビをつけたままにしておく	leave the TV on	
よく使う！ □ テレビを消す	turn off the TV	switch off the TVとも言います。

TV＋名詞

□ テレビタレント	TV personality	talentは「才能」という意味。TV talentとも言います。
□ ケーブル[有線]テレビ	cable TV	
□ テレビ〈の受像機〉	TV set	

Key word: movie [múːvi] 名 映画　CD1-83

動詞＋movie

よく使う！ □ 映画を観に行く	go to a movie	どの映画を見るかを決めているときはthe movie、決めていないときはa movieとします。複数の映画を見るならmovies。
□ 映画を封切る	release a movie	
□ 映画を上映する	show a movie	

□ 映画を製作する	produce a movie

形容詞 / 分詞 ＋ movie

□ ヒット映画	**hit** movie	successful movieでもOK。
□〈飛行機の〉機内映画	**in-flight** movie	
□ 深夜映画	**late-night** movie	
□ 成人向け映画	**X-rated** movie	

movie ＋名詞

□ 映画監督	movie **director**	
□ 映画館 *よく使う!*	movie **theater**	cinemaとも言います。
□ 映画スター	movie **star**	

例文 重要会話フレーズで覚えよう！ CD1 84

Turn off the TV before you go to bed.
（寝る前にテレビを消しなさい）

How about **going to a movie** this evening?
（今晩、映画を観に行かない？）

The director's latest **movie** will be **released** next month.
（その監督の最新映画が来月封切になる）

Keyword: **party** [pá:rti] 名 パーティー

動詞 + party

□ パーティーを開く	**hold** a party	have[give/throw] a party でもOK。
□ パーティーの手配をする	**arrange** a party	
□ パーティーのホスト役を務める	**host** a party	

名詞 + party

□ 忘年会	**year-end** party	end-of-the-year partyとも言います。「新年会」は New Year('s) party。
□ 送別会 〔よく使う!〕	**farewell** party	
□ 歓迎会 〔よく使う!〕	**welcome** party	bachelorは「独身男性」。アメリカでは結婚前（夜）に花婿と男性の友人たちがパーティーを開く習慣があります。
□ 飲み会	**drinking** party	
□ 男性だけのパーティー	**bachelor** party	
□ 立食パーティー	**stand-up** party	potluckの語源はpot（なべ）+luck（運）です。
□ 食べ物持ち寄りのパーティー	**potluck** party	

例文 重要会話フレーズで覚えよう！

Let's **have a welcome party** for him.
（彼の歓迎会を開こう）

Others その他

動詞＋名詞

- □ 〜の誕生日を祝う　**celebrate 〜 's birthday**
  > 「誕生日おめでとう」はHappy birthday!、「婚約おめでとう」はCongratulations on your engagement! と言います。
- □ 時間をつぶす　**kill time**
- □ トランプ遊びをする　**play cards**
- □ 〜の手相を見る　**read 〜 's palm**
- □ 〜の運勢を占う　**tell 〜 's fortune**
  > 「占い師」はfortune-teller。
- □ くじを引く　**draw a lot**
- □ 大当たりする　**hit a jackpot**

例文 重要会話フレーズで覚えよう！

I killed time reading comics.
（マンガを読んで時間をつぶした）

I had my fortune told.
（占いをしてもらいました）

Let me read your palm.
（手相を見てあげよう）

Scene 12
外で遊ぶ

海や山で遊ぼう!

Key word: **camp** [kǽmp]
名 キャンプ
動 キャンプする

CD1 89

動詞 + camping

- □ キャンプに行く (よく使う!) **go camping**

camping + 名詞

- □ キャンプ場　**camping area** — campsiteとも言います。
- □ キャンプ用具　**camping equipment**
- □ 飯ごう　**camping pot** — 「寝袋」は sleeping bag。
- □ 林間学校　**camping school**

Key word: **fire** [fáiər]
名 火

CD1 90

動詞 + fire

- □ 火をおこす　**make a fire** — build a fireでもOK。
- □ 火がつく　**catch fire**
- □ 火を消す　**put out the fire** — extinguish the fireでもOK。(fire)extinguisherは「消火器」。

☐ たきぎに火をつける	set fire to the wood	

fire ＋動詞

☐ 火の勢いが弱まった。	The fire died down.	
☐ 火がくすぶっている。	The fire is smoldering.	
☐ **よく使う！** 火が消えた。	The fire went out.	「火」は数えられませんが、火事やたき火は数えられるのでa fireと言います。
☐ **間違えやすい！** 火事が起きた。	A fire broke out.	

fire ＋名詞

☐ 火災報知機	fire alarm
☐ 消火 [避難] 訓練	fire drill
☐ 消防車	fire engine
☐ 消防署	fire station

例文 重要会話フレーズで覚えよう！　CD1 91

We went camping by a lake.
（湖のほとりへキャンプに行きました）

Let's make a fire before it gets dark.
（暗くならないうちに火をおこそう）

Others その他

動詞＋名詞	
□ ハイキングに行く	go on a hike
□ ピクニックに行く	go on a picnic
□ 花見に行く	go (and) see cherry blossoms
□ イチゴ狩りに行く	go (and) pick strawberries
□ ホタル狩りに行く	go (and) catch fireflies
□ 潮干狩りに行く	go (and) dig for clams
□ 釣りに行く	go fishing
□ 雪だるまを作る	make a snowman
□ 雪合戦をする	have a snowball fight
□ 神社にお参りする	visit a shrine
□ おみくじを引く	consult an oracle
□ テントを張る	pitch a tent

> ハイキングは歩くこと、ピクニックはお弁当を食べることが主な目的です。

> 「父の墓参をする」はvisit one's father's tomb。

> 「テントをたたむ」はfold up a tent。

□ マッチをする	strike a match
□ ボートをこぐ	row a boat
□ たこを揚げる	fly a kite
□ さいころを転がす	roll dice
□ ブランコに乗る	sit in a swing
□ 縄跳びをする	jump rope
□ かけっこをする	run a race
□ 馬に乗る	ride a horse

> 「こまを回す」はspin a top、「シャボン玉を吹く」はblow bubbles。

> 「すべり台で遊ぶ」はplay on a slide、「シーソーをする」はplay on a seesaw。

> 「位置について、用意、ドン！」はOn your mark, get set, go!と言います。

例文 重要会話フレーズで覚えよう！ CD1 93

We'll go see cherry blossoms in the park next Sunday.
（今度の日曜日に公園へ花見に行きます）

Let's go fishing in the river.
（川へ魚釣りに行こう）

I visited the shrine and prayed for success in business.
（神社にお参りして商売繁盛を祈願した）

形容詞 / 分詞 / 名詞＋名詞

☐ 遊園地	**amusement park**	
☐ 入場料	**entrance fee**	admission chargeとも言います。
☐ ジェットコースター【間違えやすい!】	**roller coaster**	「ジェットコースター」は和製英語です。「観覧車」はFerris wheel、「迷路」はmaze、「ろう人形」はwax doll。
☐ お化け屋敷	**haunted house**	
☐ 仮装行列	**fancy-dress parade**	
☐ おみこし	**portable shrine**	
☐ 縁日	**day of the fair**	「屋台」はstall。
☐ 花火大会	**fireworks display**	
☐ 夜店	**night fair**	「金魚すくいをする」はscoop goldfish。
☐ 流れ星	**shooting star**	「星が流れた」はA star shot、「天体観測」はstargazing。
☐ 避暑地；夏の行楽地	**summer resort**	
☐ 温泉	**hot spa**	hot springでもOK。
☐ みやげ物店	**souvenir shop**	

☐ 展望台	**observation deck**	「海水浴に行く」はgo swimming in the sea。
☐ 海水浴	**sea bathing**	
☐ 海水浴場	**swimming beach**	bathing beachでもOK。「水着」はswimsuit。
☐ ビーチパラソル	**beach umbrella**	
☐ スイカ割り	**watermelon cracking**	
☐ 温水プール	**heated pool**	
☐ 潮の干満	**ebb and flow**	

例文 重要会話フレーズで覚えよう!

How about riding the roller coaster?
(ジェットコースターに乗らない?)

The entrance fee is $1.50 per head.
(入場料金は1人当たり1ドル50セントです)

Today is the day of the fair.
(今日は縁日です)

A night fair is held in this square every Saturday.
(この広場では毎週土曜日に夜店が開かれる)

Young men are carrying a portable shrine on their shoulders.
(若者たちがおみこしをかついでいる)

Scene 13 ドライブ

ドライブに連れて行って!

Key word: car [káːr] 名 車

動詞 + car

よく使う！ 車を運転する	drive a car	
車をバックさせる	back a car up	get intoでもOK。「車から降りる」はget out of a car。バスなど大型の車の場合は、get on（乗る）、get off（降りる）を使います。
車をぶつける	hit a car	
間違えやすい！ 車に乗り込む	get in a car	
車のエンジンをかける	start up a car	
給油する	fill up a car	refill the tankとも言います。飲み物の「お代わり」もrefillです。
よく使う！ 駐車する	park a car	
よく使う！ 車を修理する	repair a car	
車を牽引[レッカー移動]する	tow a car	「車検」はcar[safety] inspection。
車を点検する	inspect a car	

car ＋動詞	
間違えやすい！ 車がスリップした。	**My car skidded.**　My car slipped. とは言いません。
車が（へいに）衝突した。	**The car crashed (into the wall).**
車は右折した。	**The car turned right.**

形容詞 / 名詞＋ car	
オートマ車	**automatic car**
国産車	**domestic car**
燃費のよい車	**fuel-efficient car**
レンタカー	**rental car**
スポーツカー	**sports car**
パトカー	**patrol car**

「マニュアルの車」はstick shift、またはcar with a manual transmission。

「この車は燃費がいい」はThis car gets good mileage。「省エネ車」はenergy-saving car。

car ＋名詞	
カーポート	**car port**　屋根つきの自動車置き場のこと。
カープール	**car pool**　自家用車に相乗りして通勤すること。

Scene 11 家で遊ぶ

Scene 12 外で遊ぶ

Scene 13 ドライブ

Scene 14 旅行

Scene 15 健康

Key word: **drive** [dráiv] 名 ドライブ 動 運転する

動詞 + drive

☐ ドライブに出かける 間違えやすい!	go for a drive	go drivingとは言いません。
☐ ドライブをする	take a drive	
☐ 〜をドライブに連れて行く	take 〜 for a drive	

形容詞 + driving

☐ 飲酒運転	drunk driving	
☐ 安全運転	safe driving	「安全運転をする」はdrive safely。
☐ 無謀運転	reckless driving	「彼は運転が上手だ」は He's a good driver. と言います。
☐ 運転が得意だ	be good at driving	

drive + 名詞など

☐ 車で通勤する	drive to work	
☐ 友人を車で家まで送る	drive a friend home	「友人を車で迎えに行く」はpick up a friend。
☐ 車で帰宅する	drive home	

例文 重要会話フレーズで覚えよう！ CD1-98

Can I park my car here?
(ここに駐車してもいいですか)

My car is being repaired at the garage.
(私の車は修理工場で修理中です)

I'm looking for a gas station to refill the tank.
(ガソリンを入れるためにガソリンスタンドを探しています)

I'll have my car inspected at the garage.
(車を車検に出します)

I crashed my car into a telephone pole.
(私は車を電柱にぶつけた)

I found that my car had been towed away.
(私の車はレッカー移動されていた)

Let's go for a drive to the beach.
(海岸へドライブに行こう)

Take me for a drive to the beach.
(海岸へドライブに連れて行ってよ)

We took a long drive to the country last Sunday.
(私たちは先週の日曜日に車で田舎へ遠出しました)

I got caught for drunk driving.
(飲酒運転でつかまった)

I made a detour to drive her home.
(私は彼女を車で家へ送るために回り道をした)

Others その他

動詞＋名詞

□ パンクする **よく使う!**	get a flat	flat = flat tire（平らな[ぺちゃんこの]タイヤ）。
□ ハンドルを切る	turn the wheel	
□ スピードを落とす	slow down (the speed)	「スピードを上げる」はspeed up。
□ クラクションを鳴らす	blow a horn	honk a hornでもOK。
□ 免停になる	have one's driver's license suspended	

形容詞／分詞／名詞＋名詞

□ バックミラー **間違えやすい!**	rearview mirror	「バック」をそのままbackとしないように注意。
□ 追い越し車線	passing lane	fast laneでもOK。「高速道路」はexpressway。
□ 駐車場	parking lot	
□ ガソリンスタンド	gas station	
□ 駐車違反	illegal parking	
□ 速度違反摘発装置	speed trap	「スピード違反」は speeding。

こんなに違う！部分の名称

車の部分を表す英語（特にアメリカ英語）は、日本語のカタカナとは違うものが多いので注意しましょう。

「サイドミラー」➡ sideview mirror
「ハンドル」➡ (steering) wheel
「フロントガラス」➡ windshield
「ナンバープレート」➡ license plate
「ボンネット」➡ hood
「ウインカー（方向指示ランプ）」➡ blinkers

例文 重要会話フレーズで覚えよう！

I got a flat in the middle of the road.
（道路の真ん中でパンクした）

The driver turned the wheel to the right.
（運転手はハンドルを右に切った）

I had my driver's license suspended [canceled] for speeding.
（スピード違反で免停［免許取り消し］になった）

There is a parking lot at the back of this building.
（この建物の裏に駐車場があります）

I was fined for illegal parking.
（駐車違反で罰金を取られた）

Scene 14 旅行

切符を買って旅に出よう

Key word: **ticket** [tíkit] 名 切符；券

動詞 + ticket

- [ ] 切符を見せる　**show a ticket**
- [ ] （〜に）切符を手渡す　**hand over a ticket (to 〜)**
- [ ] 切符の払い戻しを受ける　**get a refund on one's ticket**

形容詞 / 名詞 + ticket

- [ ] 片道切符　**one-way ticket**　 よく使う!
- [ ] 往復切符　**round-trip ticket**　 よく使う!
- [ ] 無効の切符　**invalid ticket** 　＊validは「有効な」。
- [ ] 定期[回数]券　**commuter ticket**
- [ ] 回数券　**coupon ticket**
- [ ] 周遊券　**excursion ticket**
- [ ] 入場券　**admission ticket**

☐ 宝くじ	**lottery** ticket	
☐ 当たりくじ	**winning** ticket	
☐ 食券	**meal** ticket	

ticket ＋名詞

☐ 改札口	ticket **gate**	改札口や切符売り場の窓口は **wicket** とも言います。
☐ 切符販売機	ticket **machine**	
☐ 切符売り場	ticket **office**	
☐ 集札係	ticket **collector**	

例文 重要会話フレーズで覚えよう！

I got a full refund on my ticket.
（切符を全額払い戻してもらった）

I bought two round-trip tickets to Boston.
（ボストンまでの往復切符を2枚買った）

This excursion ticket is valid for two weeks.
（この周遊券は2週間有効です）

May I ask where the ticket office is?
（切符売り場はどちらでしょうか）

Key word: **tour** [túər] 名 旅行

※tourは「小旅行；周遊旅行」。tripは長い旅行にも短い旅行にも使います。travelやjourneyは長期間または遠距離の旅行を指します。

動詞 + tour

□ 旅行をする	**take** a tour	make a tourでもOK。
□ 旅行の手配をする	**arrange** a tour	
□ 旅行を中止する	**cancel** a tour	
□ ツアーに加わる	**join** a tour	

形容詞 / 分詞 / 名詞 + tour

□ 世界一周旅行	**around-the-world** tour	
□ パックツアー	**package** tour	希望者が追加料金を払って参加するツアーは optional tour。
□ ガイドつきの旅行	**guided** tour	

例文 重要会話フレーズで覚えよう！

I'm planning to take a tour of Europe.
(ヨーロッパ旅行を計画中です)

I joined a package tour to South Korea.
(韓国へのパックツアーに参加した)

Key word: **film** [fílm] 名 フィルム

動詞＋film

- フィルムを入れる — **load** (the) film
- フィルムを現像する — **develop** (the) film
- フィルムを焼く[印刷する] — **print** (the) film

> DPEはdeveloping（現像）、printing（焼き付け）、enlarging（引き伸ばし）の頭文字を取った和製英語。「写真を焼く[印刷する]」はprint (the) picture。

名詞＋film

- 1本のフィルム — **a roll of** film
- 24枚撮りのフィルム — **24-exposure** film

film＋動詞

- フィルムが詰まった。 — The film has **jammed**.

例文 重要会話フレーズで覚えよう！

I forgot to load film in my camera.
=I fogot to load my camera with film.
（カメラにフィルムを入れ忘れた）

This roll of film has 24 exposures.
（このフィルムは24枚撮りです）

I'll have two copies of this picture printed.
（この写真を2枚焼いてもらいます）

Key word: seat [síːt] 名 席

動詞 + seat

□ 席を予約する **よく使う!**	reserve a seat	book a seatでもOK。「指定席」はreserved seat。「自由席」はnon-reserved seat。
□ 席〈の予約〉を取る	get a seat	
□ 席を替わる	change seats	
□ 席を譲る	offer one's seat	
□ シートベルトを締める	fasten one's seat belt	

形容詞 / 名詞 + seat

□ 通路側の席	aisle seat	「窓際の席」はwindow seat。
□ 空席 **よく使う!**	empty seat	vacant seatでもOK。
□ 〈車の〉前の座席; 助手席	front seat	後部座席はback [rear] seat。
□ 〈劇場などの〉最前列の席	front-row seats	

例文 重要会話フレーズで覚えよう!

There were no empty seats on the bus.
(バスには空席がなかった)

A young boy offered his seat to the old man.
(若者がその老人に席を譲った)

Key word: **photo** [fóutou] 名 写真

※photoはphotographの短縮形。スナップ写真はshotとも言います。

動詞 + photo

- [ ] 写真を撮る　　**take** a photo
- [ ] 写真を引き伸ばす　**enlarge** a photo

☞ photoはshotやpictureでもOK。

Others: その他

形容詞 / 分詞 / 名詞 + 名詞

- [ ] 旅行代理店　　**travel agency**
- [ ] 〈ホテルの〉フロント　**front desk** 〔間違えやすい！〕
- [ ] キャンセル待ち名簿　**waiting list**

☞ 単にfrontでは意味が通じません。

例文　重要会話フレーズで覚えよう！

Excuse me, could you take a photo of us?
（すみません、私たちの写真を撮っていただけますか）

Let's take a souvenir shot in front of that statue.
（あの像の前で記念写真を撮ろうよ）

We're on the waiting list of the flight.
（私たちはその便のキャンセル待ちです）

Scene 11 家で遊ぶ / Scene 12 外で遊ぶ / Scene 13 ドライブ / Scene 14 旅行 / Scene 15 健康

Scene 15
健康

健康増進のために運動！

Key word: **sport** [spɔ́ːrt] 名 スポーツ

動詞 + sport

□ スポーツをする（よく使う！）	do sports	play sports とも言います。
□ スポーツを始める	take up a sport	

形容詞 / 名詞 + sport

□ 屋内のスポーツ	indoor sports	「屋外のスポーツ」はoutdoor sports。
□ 国技	national sports	
□ 個人競技	individual sports	「団体競技」は team sports。
□ 私の好きなスポーツ	my favorite sports	
□ 人気のあるスポーツ	popular sports	
□ 大勢の観客を集めるスポーツ	spectator sports	
□ 陸上競技	athletic sports	athleteは「運動選手」。
□ 格闘技	combat sports	空手・柔道などの「武道」は martial arts。

sports ＋名詞	
□ スポーツ施設	**sports facility**
□ スポーツ用品	**sports equipment**
□ スポーツ大会	**sports event**
□〈学校の〉運動会	**sports day**
□ 運動靴	**sports shoes**
□ スポーツ新聞	**sports paper**

☞ public facility は「公共施設」。

☞ sports gear でもOK。

例文 重要会話フレーズで覚えよう！

Do you do any sports?
（何かスポーツをしていますか）

I want to take up a sport to improve my health.
（健康のためにスポーツを始めたい）

Sumo is Japan's national sport.
（相撲は日本の国技です）

My town doesn't have enough sports facilities.
（私の町には十分なスポーツ施設がない）

The children are looking forward to the sports day.
（子供たちは運動会を楽しみにしている）

Key word: **health** [hélθ] 名 健康

CD2-16

動詞 + health

□ 健康を保つ (よく使う!)	**keep** one's health	keep fit、stay healthyとも言います。
□ 健康を増進する	**improve** one's health	
□ 健康を損なう	**damage** one's health	lose one's healthでもOK。
□ 健康を取り戻す	**recover** one's health	

health + 名詞

□ 健康保険	health **insurance**	「健康保険証」は health insurance card。
□ ヘルスクラブ	health **club**	
□ 健康ランド	health **spa**	physical[medical] checkupとも言います。「人間ドック」は thorough checkup。
□ 健康診断	health **examination**	

例文 重要会話フレーズで覚えよう！

CD2-17

You need to get a health examination regularly.
（定期的に健康診断を受けたほうがいいよ）

I have national health insurance.
（私は国民健康保険に入っています）

Key word: **exercise** [éksərsàiz] 名 運動

動詞 + exercise	
□ 運動する	**do** exercise

get[take] exerciseでもOK。

形容詞 / 名詞 + exercise	
□ 体操	**physical** exercise
□ 腹筋運動	**abdominal** exercise
□ 準備運動	**warm-up** exercise
□ 激しい運動	**hard** exercise
□ 適度な運動	**moderate** exercise
□ 過度の運動	**excessive** exercise
□ 運動不足	**lack of** exercise

「腹筋」は abdominal muscles。

例文 重要会話フレーズで覚えよう！

It's good for your health to get moderate exercise.
(適度な運動をするのは健康によい)

My muscles have weakened due to lack of exercise.
(運動不足で筋肉が弱くなった)

Key word: smoking [smóukiŋ] 名 喫煙　CD2-20

動詞 ＋ smoking

よく使う！ 禁煙する	stop smoking	give up smoking でもOK。
喫煙を控える	refrain from smoking	「受動［間接］喫煙」はpassive smoking。「副流煙」はsecondhand smoke。
喫煙を禁じる	prohibit smoking	

smoking ＋ 名詞

喫煙コーナー	smoking area	「禁煙車両」はnonsmoking car。
〈電車の〉喫煙車両	smoking car	

Others その他　CD2-21

動詞 ＋ 名詞 / 形容詞

よく使う！ 減量する	lose weight	「体重が増える」は gain [put on] weight。
よく使う！ ダイエットをする	go on a diet	「ダイエット中だ」は be on a diet。
体力を維持する	keep up one's strength	sit-upは「腹筋運動」、chin-upは「（鉄棒の）懸垂」。
腕立て伏せをする	do a push-up	

☐ 筋肉を鍛える	strengthen one's muscles	
☐ 握力が強い	have a strong grip	
☐ エアロビクスをする	do aerobics	
☐ ジョギングに行く	go for a jog	☞ I jog every day.（毎日ジョギングしている）のように動詞としても使います。
☐ たばこに火をつける	light one's cigarette	

形容詞 / 名詞＋名詞

☐ 体力	physical strength
☐ 筋力	muscular strength
☐ 肺活量	lung power
☐ たばこの吸い殻	cigarette butt

例文 重要会話フレーズで覚えよう！　CD2 22

Smoking is prohibited in this office.
（このオフィスは禁煙です）

I'm **going on a diet** to lose weight.
（減量するためにダイエットするつもりです）

I **do 50 push-ups** every day.
（私は毎日50回腕立て伏せをします）

Scene 16 散歩

犬と一緒に公園へ

Key word **walk** [wɔ́ːk] 名 歩くこと；散歩

動詞＋walk

□ 散歩をする **よく使う!**	take a walk	have a walk でもOK。
□ 散歩に行く **よく使う!**	go for a walk	
□ ペットを散歩に連れ出す	take one's pet for a walk	one's pet に限らず人物を入れてもOK。

形容詞/名詞＋walk

□ 楽しい散歩	pleasant walk	
□ 30分の散歩 **間違えやすい!**	30-minute walk	ハイフンの後ろの名詞(minute)は単数形にします。
□ 早朝の散歩	early morning walk	

例文 重要会話フレーズで覚えよう！

I'm going to the park for a walk.
（公園へ散歩に行くところです）

A 30-minute walk every day will make you stay healthy.
（毎日30分散歩すれば健康を保てます）

I took my dog for a walk.
（犬を散歩に連れ出しました）

Key word: **bicycle** [báisikl] 名 自転車

※自転車はbikeとも言います。日本語の「バイク［オートバイ］」に当たる英語は(motor)bike、motorcycleです。

動詞 + bicycle

- □ 自転車に乗る — **ride (on)** a bicycle
  - 👉 rideは乗って運転する場合に使います。「自転車にまたがる」はget on a bicycle、「自転車から降りる」はget off a bicycleです。
- □ 自転車をこぐ — **pedal** a bicycle
- □ 自転車にカギをかける — **lock** one's bicycle
- □ 貸し自転車を借りる — **rent** a bicycle
- □ 自転車を押していく — **push** a bicycle
  - 👉 walk a bicycleでもOK。
- □ 駐輪する — **park** a bicycle

bicycle + 名詞

- □ 自転車置き場 — bicycle **shed**

例文 重要会話フレーズで覚えよう！

Don't ride double on bicycles.
（自転車に二人乗りしてはいけません）

I got a flat tire and walked my bike home.
（パンクしたので自転車を押して家へ帰った）

I had my bike stolen at the bicycle shed.
（自転車置き場で自転車を盗まれた）

Key word: pet [pét] 名 ペット

CD2 27

動詞 + pet

□ ペットを飼う（よく使う！）	**keep** a pet	have a petでもOK。
□ ペットの世話をする（よく使う！）	**take care of** a pet	
□ ペットを捨てる	**abandon** a pet	

名詞 / 分詞 + pet

□ 最愛のペット	**beloved** pet	みんなにかわいがられる人［八方美人］はeverybody's petと言います。
□ 先生のお気に入り（の生徒）	**teacher's** pet	

pet + 名詞

□ ペットショップ	pet **shop**	
□ ペットフード	pet **food**	
□ ペットの美容室	pet **grooming studio**	
□ ペットの死による悲しみ	pet **loss grief**	petは「お気に入りの」の意味でも使います。his pet theoryは「彼の持論」です。
□ 口ぐせ	pet **phrase**	

Key word: **dog** [dɔ́g] 名 犬

※dogをほかのペットの名前に変えれば応用できる表現もたくさんあります。

動詞 ＋ dog

よく使う！ 犬にえさをやる	feed a dog	
犬を飼育する	raise a dog	breed a dogでもOK。breed a dogは「犬に子供を産ませる」というニュアンス。
犬に運動させる	exercise a dog	
よく使う！ 犬を散歩させる	walk a dog	
犬に芸を教える	teach a dog tricks	「お手！」はShake hands!、「おすわり！」はDown!、「おあずけ！」はWait!。
犬を呼ぶ	call a dog	
犬にトイレのしつけをする	housebreak a dog	「トイレのしつけをしてある犬[猫]」はhousebroken dog [cat] と言います。
犬をひもにつなぐ	leash a dog	
犬をなでる	pat a dog	
犬を鎖につなぐ	chain up a dog	
犬を木につなぐ	tie a dog to a tree	

☐ 犬を放してやる	let a dog loose	

dog ＋動詞

☐ **よく使う!** 犬がほえている。	The dog is barking.	ライオンなどの猛獣がほえるのはroar。
☐ 犬がうなっている。	The dog is growling.	
☐ 犬が尾を振っている。	The dog is wagging its tail.	

形容詞 / 分詞＋dog

☐ 雄犬	male dog	he-dogとも言います。「雌犬」はfemale[she-]dog。
☐ 猛犬	fierce dog	
☐ 忠犬	faithful dog	
☐ 野良犬	stray dog	ownerless [wild/homeless] dogとも言います。
☐ 猟犬	hunting dog	
☐ むく犬	shaggy dog	
☐ 盲導犬	seeing-eye dog	guide dogでもOK。
☐ 警備犬	guard dog	「番犬」はwatchdog。

dog ＋名詞	
□ 愛犬家	**dog lover**
□ 犬の鑑札	**dog tag**
□ 犬の首輪	**dog collar**
□ 乱戦 ; 空中戦	**dog fight**
□ 〈水泳の〉犬かき	**dog paddle**

例文 重要会話フレーズで覚えよう！

I have to ask someone to take care of my pet birds while I'm away.
（私は不在の間ペットの鳥の世話を誰かに頼む必要がある）

Some irresponsible people abandon their pets too easily.
（一部の無責任な人々は簡単にペットを捨てる）

I walked my dog in the park.
＝ I took my dog for a walk in the park.
（公園で犬を散歩させました）

Exercise your dog twice a day.
（1日に2回犬に運動させなさい）

The dog barked at me.
（その犬は私に向かってほえた）

The dog has a collar around its neck.
（その犬は首輪をつけている）

Scene 17 住宅

家を建てるヨ！

Key word: **house** [háus] 名 家

CD2 30

動詞 + house

□ 家を設計する	design a house	
□ 家を建てる	build a house	
□ 家をリフォームする（間違えやすい!）	remodel a house	refurbish a houseでもOK。reformは「改革する」という意味。reform a houseとは言いません。
□ 家を増築する	extend one's house	
□ 家を登記する	register a house	
□ ままごとをする	play house	

形容詞 / 分詞 / 名詞 + house

□ 建売住宅	ready-built house	「注文住宅」はcustom-built house。
□ マイホーム（間違えやすい!）	one's own house	
□ 木造の家	wooden house	「この家は木造です」はThis house is made of wood.。
□ 間取りのいい家	well-planned house	

112

□ 3階建ての家	**three-story** house	
□ 社宅	**company** house	
□ 貸家	house **for rent**	
□ お化け屋敷	**haunted** house	

housing ＋名詞

□ 住宅ローン	housing **loan**	mortgageとも言います。
□ 住宅難	housing **shortage**	

例文 重要会話フレーズで覚えよう！ CD2 31

I want to have my own house.
（私はマイホームを持ちたい）

I asked the architect to design a house for me.
（私はその建築士に家の設計を頼んだ）

The developer sells ready-built houses.
（その宅地開発業者は建売住宅を売っている）

This house is registered in the name of my wife.
（この家は妻の名義で登記してあります）

I haven't paid off my housing loan yet.
（まだ住宅ローンを返済していません）

Key word: **apartment** [əpáːrtmənt] 名 アパート

CD2-32

動詞 + apartment

- [ ] アパートを探す **look for** an apartment
- [ ] アパートを借りる **rent** an apartment 〈よく使う!〉
- [ ] アパートを(〜と)共同で使う **share** an apartment **(with 〜)**
- [ ] 新しいアパートに引っ越す **move to** a new apartment
- [ ] アパートの模様替えをする **redecorate** an apartment

形容詞 / 分詞 / 名詞 + apartment

- [ ] ワンルームマンション **studio** apartment 〈間違えやすい!〉
  - ☞ apartmentはなくてもOK。mansionは「大邸宅」のこと。
- [ ] 広々としたアパート **spacious** apartment
- [ ] 狭いアパート **small** apartment 〈間違えやすい!〉
  - ☞ narrowは「幅が狭い」。
- [ ] 家具つきのアパート **furnished** apartment
- [ ] アパートの家賃 **the rent for** an apartment
  - ☞ 敷金はdeposit。英米には礼金の習慣はありません。

apartment + 名詞

- [ ] アパート〈の建物〉 **apartment building** 〈間違えやすい!〉
  - ☞ apartmentはアパートの一世帯分のこと。

Key word: **window** [wíndou] 名 窓

動詞 ＋ window

- [ ] 窓を閉める　　**close a window**　　☞ shut a window でもOK。
- [ ] 窓ガラスを割る　**break a window**　　☞ 窓ガラスは windowpane とも言います。
- [ ] 窓ガラスをふく　**wipe a window**

形容詞 / 名詞 ＋ window

- [ ] 出窓　　　　　**bay window**
- [ ] 曇った窓　　　**misty window**　　☞ fogged window でもOK。
- [ ] ガタガタする窓 **loose window**

例文 重要会話フレーズで覚えよう！

I rent this apartment for 700 dollars a month.
（このアパートは月 700 ドルで借りています）

I live in a studio apartment.
（私はワンルームマンションに住んでいます）

How much is the monthly rent for this apartment?
（この部屋の家賃は月々いくらですか）

Wipe the windows with this rag.
（このぞうきんで窓をふきなさい）

The windows are fogged with steam.
（蒸気で窓が曇っている）

Key word: door [dɔ́ːr] 名 ドア

動詞 + door

ドアをノックする	knock on the door
ドアを開けておく	leave the door open
ドアをバタンと閉める	slam the door
ドアに鍵をかける	lock the door
ドアに鍵をかけておく	keep the door locked
ドアの鍵を開ける	unlock the door

分詞 + door

回転ドア	revolving door
障子	sliding door

例文 重要会話フレーズで覚えよう！

Someone is knocking on the door.
(誰かがドアをノックしている)

I forgot to lock the door.
(部屋に鍵をかけ忘れた)

Others その他

動詞＋名詞

芝生を刈る	cut a lawn	mow a lawnでもOK。
芝生の雑草を取る	weed a lawn	
庭に水をまく	water a garden	
生け垣を刈り込む	trim a hedge	
種をまく	plant seeds	

名詞＋動詞

屋根が雨漏りする。	The roof leaks.
階段がぎしぎし鳴る。	The stairs creak.

形容詞／名詞＋名詞

火災保険	insurance against fire

「保険証書」は insurance policy。insure ～ against fire で「～に火災保険をかける」。

例文 重要会話フレーズで覚えよう！

My house is insured against fire.
（わが家は火災保険に入っています）

I planted watermelon seeds in my garden.
（庭にスイカの種をまいた）

Scene 18 家事

洗濯物を取り込んで！

Key word: **room** [rú:m] 名 部屋

動詞 ＋ room	
よく使う！ 部屋をきれいに掃除する	clean up a room
部屋を片付ける	tidy (up) a room
(〜のために) 場所をあける	make room (for 〜)

形容詞 / 名詞 ＋ room	
よく使う！ 散らかった部屋	messy room
ほこりっぽい部屋	dusty room
6畳間	six-mat room
部屋の寸法	the dimensions of a room

「この部屋はひどく散らかっている」はThis room is a terrible [awful] mess. と言います。

dustは「ちり；ほこり」、dusterは「ぞうきん；はたき」。

例文 重要会話フレーズで覚えよう！

We have a ten-mat living room.
(わが家の居間は10畳です)

Key word **floor** [flɔ́:r] 名 床

動詞＋ floor

□ 床を掃く	**sweep** the floor	「ほうき」は broom、「ちり取り」は dustpan。
□ 床にモップをかける	**mop** the floor	
□ 床を磨く	**polish** the floor	
□ 床をふく	**wipe** the floor	
□ 床に電気掃除機をかける〈よく使う！〉	**vacuum** the floor	vacuumは vacuum cleaner（真空[電気]掃除機）からきた動詞。
□ 床にワックスをかける	**wax** the floor	

形容詞＋ floor

□〈建物の〉1階	**the first** floor	イギリス英語では「1階」は ground floor。
□ 上の階	**upper** floor	

例文 重要会話フレーズで覚えよう！

Wipe the floor with a rag after **sweeping** it.
（床を掃いたあと、ぞうきんでふきなさい）

My office is on **the eighth floor**.
（私のオフィスは8階にあります）

Key word: laundry [lɔ́:ndri] 名 洗濯(物)

動詞 + laundry

☐ 洗濯をする	do the laundry	do the washing も「洗濯する」という意味。
☐ 洗濯物を乾かす	dry the laundry	「洗濯(物)」は washing とも言います。
☐ 洗濯物を〈つるして〉干す	hang out the laundry (to dry)	
☐ 洗濯物を取り込む	bring the laundry in	bring は自分が家の中にいるときに使う表現。外にいるときには take を使います。
☐ 洗濯物をたたむ	fold the laundry	
☐ 洗濯物にアイロンをかける	iron the laundry	「アイロン台」は ironing board [table]。
☐ 洗濯物をクリーニングに出す	send out the laundry	

形容詞 + laundry

☐ 汚れた洗濯物	dirty laundry
☐ ぬれた洗濯物	wet laundry

例文 重要会話フレーズで覚えよう！

It looks like rain. Bring the laundry in.
(雨が降りそう。洗濯物を取り込んで)

I do the laundry at a laundromat.
(私はコインランドリーで洗濯をします)

Key word: **garbage** [gáːrbidʒ] 名 ごみ

※台所から出る生ごみはgarbage、乾いたごみ（道路や公園などに散らかっているごみなど）はtrashです。イギリスではごみ全般をrabbishと言います。以下の例の多くは、garbageの代わりにtrashも使えます。

動詞 + garbage

よく使う！ ごみを出す	**take out** garbage	put out garbage でもOK。
ごみを捨てる	**dump** garbage	throw out garbageでもOK。
ごみを回収する	**collect** garbage	
ごみを分別する	**separate** garbage	

形容詞 / 分詞 + bargabe

よく使う！ 燃えるごみ	**burnable** garbage	「燃えないごみ」は unburnalbe [nonburnable] garbage。
未回収のごみ	**uncollected** garbage	garbage collector [man] は「ごみ回収作業員」。
ごみの山	**piled** garbage	

garbage + 名詞

生ごみ入れ	garbage **can**	garbage pail でもOK。公園などのくずかごは trash can。
ごみ袋	garbage **bag**	
ごみ回収車	garbage **truck**	

Others その他

動詞＋名詞

□ 掃除をする	do the cleaning
□ しみをつける	leave a stain
□ しみ[汚れ]を落とす	remove a stain
□ バケツをひっくり返す	turn over a bucket
□ 水を出しっ放しにする	leave the water running

形容詞／名詞＋名詞

□ 大掃除	house cleaning
□ 掃除用具	cleaning equipment
□ 粗大ごみ	bulky refuse
□ 洗濯機	washing machine
□ 肌に優しい洗剤	mild detergent
□ ぬるま湯	lukewarm water
□ 給水	water supply

例文　重要会話フレーズで覚えよう！　CD2-47

On which days should I take out burnable garbage?
(燃えるごみは何曜日に出せばいいですか)

They collect garbage by type in this town.
(この町ではごみを分別回収しています)

Separate the trash before throwing it out.
(ごみを出す前に分別しなさい)

The garbage truck comes around at about 8:00.
(ごみ回収車は8時ごろ回って来ます)

Put the empty can into that trash can.
(空き缶はあのごみ箱に入れなさい)

I spilled my coffee and left a stain on the carpet.
(私はコーヒーをこぼしてカーペットにしみをつけた)

We did the general house cleaning last Sunday.
(先週の日曜日に家の大掃除をしました)

The washing machine is out of order.
(洗濯機は故障している)

Soak the laundry in lukewarm water.
(洗濯物をぬるま湯に浸けておきなさい)

The water supply has been cut off.
(断水している)

Scene 19 食事

産地直送ってどう表現？

Key word: **food** [fúːd] 名 食べ物；食品

CD2 48

動詞 + food

よく使う！ □ 食べ物を〈お客に〉出す	**serve** food
よく使う！ □ 食べ物を温める	**heat up** food
□ 食べ物を冷凍する	**freeze** food
□ 食品を保存する	**preserve** food

☞「冷凍食品」は frozen food。「解凍する」は thaw [defrost]。

food + 動詞

□ 食べ物が腐った。	The food **has gone bad**.
□ この食べ物は一晩もたないだろう。	This food **won't keep overnight**.

形容詞 / 分詞 + food

□ 産地直送の食品	**farm-fresh** food
□ 健康によい食べ物	**healthy** food
間違えやすい！ □ 主食	**staple** food

☞ food fresh from the farm とも言います。

☐ 加工食品	**processed** food	food processor は肉・野菜などを切ったり混ぜたりする道具。
☐ 調理済み食品	**precooked** food	
☐ 遺伝子組み替え食品	**GM** food	= genetically-modified food の略。
☐ 輸入食品	**imported** food	
☐ 中華料理	**Chinese** food	

food ＋名詞

☐ 食品添加物	food **additive**	「無添加の」は additive-free。
☐ 食中毒	food **poisoning**	

例文 重要会話フレーズで覚えよう！ CD2 49

That restaurant serves Thai food.
（あのレストランはタイ料理を出す）

I'll heat up some food before the kids return.
（子供たちが戻る前に食べ物を温めておこう）

Rice is the staple food of the Japanese.
= **The Japanese live on rice.**
（米は日本人の主食です）

This food is free from additives.
（この食品には添加物は含まれていません）

Key word: **meat** [míːt] 名 肉

動詞 + meat

肉を〈オーブンや直火で〉焼く	**roast** meat	grilled sauryは「サンマの塩焼き」。
肉を〈網で〉焼く	**grill** meat	
肉を切り分ける	**carve** meat	肉を切るナイフはcarving knifeまたはcarver。

形容詞 + meat

生肉	**raw** meat	
硬い肉 【間違えやすい!】	**tough** meat	hard [soft] meatとは言いません。
柔らかい肉 【間違えやすい!】	**tender** meat	
赤身の肉	**lean** meat	「脂身」はfat (meat)。
霜降り肉	**marbled** meat	
ひき肉	**ground** meat	groundはgrind（ひく）の過去分詞。

例文 重要会話フレーズで覚えよう！

Would you carve the meat for us, please?
（肉を切り分けてもらえますか）

This beef is too tough to bite off.
（この牛肉は硬すぎて噛み切れない）

Key word: **table** [téibl] 名 テーブル；食卓

動詞 + table

- **よく使う!** 食卓の用意をする — **set** the table
  - ☞ lay [spread] the tableとも言います。
- **よく使う!** 食卓を片付ける — **clear** the table
- テーブルをふく — **wipe** the table
- **よく使う!** テーブルを予約する — **reserve** a table
- 相席になる — **share** the table

形容詞 / 名詞 + table

- 食卓 — **dining** table
- 丸いテーブル — **round** table
- 四角いテーブル — **square** table

例文　重要会話フレーズで覚えよう！

Can you help me set the table for the party?
(パーティーの食卓の用意をするのを手伝ってくれない？)

I'd like to reserve a table for four.
(4人掛けのテーブルを予約したいのですが)

We shared the table with another group at the restaurant.
(私たちはレストランで別のグループと相席になった)

Others その他

動詞＋名詞		
キャベツをきざむ	shred cabbage	「薄切りにする」は slice、「みじん切りにする」は mince、「さいの目切りにする」は cube。
野菜をいためる	(stir-)fry vegetables	
リンゴの皮をむく	pare an apple	pareは刃物を使う場合に使います。「手で皮をむく」はpeel。
米をとぐ	wash rice	
サラダを作る（間違えやすい！）	fix salad	make salad でもOK。
湯をわかす	boil water	
魚をさばく	clean fish	「うろこを取る」はscale、「三枚におろす」はfillet、「はらわたを出す」はgut。
スープの味見をする	taste the soup	
乾杯する	make a toast	「乾杯」のかけ声はBottoms up!やCheers!やHere's to ～! などと言います。
サラダを小皿に取り分ける	dish out the salad	
食欲がない	have no appetite	
～に夕食をおごる	treat ～ to dinner	

☐ 二日酔いだ	have a hangover	

形容詞 / 名詞＋名詞

☐ 食物繊維	dietary fiber	
☐ 有機野菜	organic vegetables	
☐ 食べ放題のレストラン	all-you-can-eat restaurant	
☐ バイキング形式のレストラン	smorgasbord restaurant	buffet-style restaurantでもOK。
☐ 回転ずしの店	conveyor-belt sushi bar	「回転ずし」はmerry-go-round（回転木馬）になぞらえてsushi-go-roundとも言います。
☐ ジョッキ1杯のビール	a mug of beer	
☐ 飲み友達	drinking buddy	

例文 重要会話フレーズで覚えよう！

Can you pare an apple with a knife?
（ナイフでリンゴの皮をむけますか）

This fruit is rich in dietary fiber.
（この果物には食物繊維が豊富です）

I drank three mugs of beer.
（ビールをジョッキ3杯飲んだ）

Here's to our reunion!
（私たちの再会を祝して乾杯！）

Scene 20 入浴・就寝

お風呂に入ってぐっすり眠ろう

Key word	**bath** [bǽθ] 名 風呂		

動詞＋bath

□ 風呂に湯を入れる	run a bath	fill a bath with waterとも表現できます。
□ 風呂をわかす 【間違えやすい!】	get a bath ready	
□ 風呂の湯加減をみる	test a bath	have a bathでもOK。「シャワーを浴びる」はtake [have] a shower。
□ 入浴する 【よく使う!】	take a bath	
□ ～を風呂に入れる	give ～ a bath	
□ 風呂の湯を流す	let a bath drain out	empty a bathとも言います。
□ 浴槽を洗う	clean a bath	

形容詞／名詞＋bath

□ 温浴	hot bath	cold bathは「冷水浴」。
□ 公衆浴場	public bath	「男[女]湯」はmen's [women's] sectionと言います。
□ 露天風呂	open-air bath	

□ 泡風呂	**bubble** bath	
□ 蒸し風呂	**steam** bath	
□ フルバス	**full** bath	

家の広告などで使う言葉で、シャワー・浴槽・便器・洗面台がそろっている浴室のことです。便器と洗面台だけの場合は half bath と言います。

bath ＋名詞	
□ バスタオル	bath **towel**
□ 入浴剤	bath **additive**

bath agent でもOK。

例文 重要会話フレーズで覚えよう！ CD2 57

I'll get the bath ready before you're back.
(あなたが戻る前にお風呂をわかしておきますね)

The bath is ready.
(お風呂がわきました)

I like taking a bath in the morning.
(朝風呂に入るのが好きです)

Help me give the baby a bath.
(赤ちゃんをお風呂に入れるのを手伝って)

Everyone has taken a bath except you.
(あなた以外はみんなお風呂を使ったわ)

Pull the plug after you've had your bath.
(出たらお湯の栓を抜いておいてね)

Dry yourself with this bath towel.
(このバスタオルで体をふきなさい)

Key word: sleep [slíːp] 名 睡眠

CD2 58

動詞 + sleep

□ 寝つく	go to sleep	「眠り込む」は fall asleep。
□ 〜を寝かしつける	put 〜 to sleep	
□ 〜の眠りを妨げる	disturb 〜 's sleep	「いびきをかく」は snore、「歯ぎしりをする」は grind one's teeth。
□ 寝言を言う	talk in one's sleep	
□ ぐっすり眠る (よく使う!)	have a good sleep	

形容詞 / 名詞 + sleep

□ 熟睡	deep sleep	sound sleep でもOK。
□ 浅い眠り	light sleep	
□ 冬眠	winter sleep	「冬眠する」は hibernate。

例文 重要会話フレーズで覚えよう！

CD2 59

My sleep was disturbed by the noise.
（物音で私の眠りは破られた）

Put the children to sleep.
（子どもたちを寝かしつけなさい）

I'm a light sleeper.
（私は眠りが浅いんです）

Key word: **light** [láit] 名 明かり

動詞 + light

□ 明かりをつける	turn on the light	put out the lightとも言います。
□ 明かりを消す	turn off the light	
□ 照明を暗くする	turn down the light	「照明を明るくする」はturn up the light。
□ 明かりをつけっ放しにする	leave the lights on	

light + 動詞

□ 明かりがついた。	The light came on.
□ 明かりが消えた。	The light went out.

形容詞 / 名詞 + light

□ 蛍光灯	fluorescent light	
□ まぶしい光	dazzling light	「薄暗い光」はdim light。

light + 名詞

□ 電球	light bulb

例文 重要会話フレーズで覚えよう！

The light bulb has burned out.
（電球が切れた）

Key word: **bed** [béd] 名 ベッド

CD2 62

動詞＋ bed		
□ 寝る よく使う!	**go to** bed	
□ 〜をベッドに連れていく	**put** 〜 **to** bed	
□ 寝たままでいる	**stay in** bed	「病気で寝ている」は be sick [ill] in bed。
□ 寝床から出る	**leave** one's bed	get out of bed とも言います。
□ 寝床を整える よく使う!	**make** a bed	
□ おねしょをする	**wet the** bed	「おねしょをする子」は bedwetter。
形容詞 / 分詞 / 名詞＋ bed		
□ 二段ベッド	**bunk** beds	
□ きしむベッド	**creaking** bed	
□ ダブルベッド	**double** bed	
□ 羽ぶとん	**feather** bed	
□ 折りたたみ式ベッド	**folding** bed	
□ 堅いベッド	**hard** bed	

Others その他

動詞＋名詞

- [ ] ふとんで寝る　　sleep on a futon
- [ ] ふとんを干す　　air out a futon
- [ ] ふとんを押し入れにしまう　　put a futon in a closet

> 敷きぶとんはmattress、掛けぶとんはquilt。

- [ ] ふとんを敷く　　spread out a futon
- [ ] ふとんをたたむ　　fold up a futon

間違えやすい!
- [ ] 悪夢を見る　　have a nightmare

> 「見る」ですがseeは使えません。

- [ ] 夢判断をする　　interpret a dream

例文 重要会話フレーズで覚えよう！

Make the bed after you get up.
（起きたあとはベッドを整えなさい）

I **stayed in bed** till noon.
（昼まで寝ていました）

It takes me ten minutes to **leave my bed** in the morning.
（私は朝寝床から出るのに10分かかります）

I **had a nightmare** last night.
（ゆうべ悪夢を見た）

コロケーション学習のコツ

　単語を学習する際に、その語を実際の英会話などで使う場合、どのような英語表現になるのか…？　こうした疑問や好奇心をもつことが、コロケーション学習の第一歩です。その状態で英和・和英辞典を使っていけば、コロケーションの知識は自然と身につき、英語の表現力はどんどん高まります。

　また、具体的な学習ツールとしては、辞典や電子辞書に加えてインターネットを活用するのがよいでしょう。ネット上に公開されている無料のオンライン辞書を使って、気になる日本語表現を検索すれば、それに相当する英語のフレーズを簡単に知ることができます。
加えて、インターネット検索は、自分の使いたい表現が英語として正しいかどうかを判断するのにも大いに役立ちます。

　たとえば「私の計算が間違っていました」という日本語を英語に直す際に、「my calculation was wrong と my calculation was mistaken のどちらがよいのか（または両方よいのか）？」という疑問を持ったとします。この場合、〈calculation was wrong〉〈calculation was mistaken〉の2つを Google などの検索エンジンで文字列検索してみるのです。すると、前者の方が圧倒的に多くヒットするので、wrong を使うべきだとわかります（実際、mistaken は人間を主語にとる形容詞なのでここでは使えません）。

　なお、ネット上の用例の中には正しくない英語も含まれています。しかしそうしたマイナス面を差し引いても、ネットから得られる情報には価値がありますので、大いに、上手に、活用しましょう。

Chapter 2

シーンにかかわらず会話で使える！
動詞+名詞の結びつき
コロケーション
200

コロケーションのうち、とくに重要なものの1つとして、「動詞+名詞」の結びつきが挙げられます。たとえば、「決心する」を1語で言うとdecideですが、make a decisionとも表現することができます（decisionは「決心」という意味の名詞）。1語で表現できるのに、なぜわざわざ長い表現を使うの…？と、思うかもしれませんが、実は英語では、「動詞+名詞」の形が好まれるのです。
ここでは、会話で非常によく使われる基本動詞を取り上げ、その中でもとくによく使われる重要な「動詞+（前置詞/副詞+）名詞」の結びつきを確認していきましょう。

have + 名詞

haveの基本的な意味は「持っている」ですが、「食べる」などの動作を表す場合にも使います。

よく使う!

☐ **have an accident** 事故にあう

例文　I had an accident on my way home from work.
（私は仕事から帰宅中に事故にあった）

よく使う!

☐ **have a baby** 出産する

＊ baby は boy や girl でも OK です。

例文　She had a boy yesterday.
（彼女はきのう男の子を出産した）

よく使う!

☐ **have a cold** 風邪をひいている

例文　I have a slight cold.
（ちょっと風邪気味です）

よく使う!

☐ **have a headache** 頭が痛い

＊「歯[胃]が痛い」は have a toothache [stomachache]。「のどが（腫れて）痛い」は have a sore throat と言います。

例文　I've had a headache since (this) morning.
（今朝からずっと頭が痛い）

動詞+名詞の結びつき**200**

よく使う!
☐ **have a fever**　熱がある

＊「熱を測る」は take one's temperature、「体温計」は thermometer です。

例文 She appears to have a fever.
= She appears to be feverish.
（彼女は熱があるみたいだ）

間違えやすい!
☐ **have a dream**　夢を見る

＊「見る」ですが see は使いませんので注意。

例文 I had a strange dream last night.
（ゆうべ変な夢を見た）

よく使う!
☐ **have lunch**　昼食をとる

例文 We had lunch at the Italian restaurant.
（私たちはイタリア料理店で昼食をとった）

☐ **have a talk**　会話する

＊ have a chat は「おしゃべりする」。

例文 We had a pleasant talk with each other.
（私たちはおたがいに楽しく語り合った）

よく使う!
☐ **have an effect on ～**　～に影響を与える

＊ have an influence on ～でも OK。

例文 His opinion had a great effect on the decision.
（彼の意見はその決定に大きな影響を与えた）

よく使う!

☐ **have a good night's sleep**　一晩ぐっすり眠る

例文　I had a good night's sleep last night.
（ゆうべはぐっすり眠りました）

☐ **have access to ～**　～が入手できる

例文　You have access to the application form on-line.
（申し込み用紙はオンラインで入手できます）

☐ **have one's (own) way**　思い通りにふるまう

例文　You shouldn't let your children have their own way all the time.
（いつも子供に思い通りにふるまわせるべきではない）

☐ **have second thoughts**　再考する

例文　We should have second thoughts about the decision.
（我々はその決定を再考するべきだ）

☐ **have ～ in common**　～を共有する

例文　The twins have many things in common.
（そのふたごには多くの共通点がある）

☐ **have ～ in mind**　～を考えて[覚えて]いる

例文　Do you have anything in mind for dinner?
（夕食に作るものを何か考えていますか）

動詞＋名詞の結びつき200

☐ **have a good time** 楽しい時を過ごす
＊形容詞を置きかえれば、have a hard [terrible] time （つらい [ひどい] 目にあう）などとも言えます。

例文 We had a good time at the party.
（パーティーで楽しい時を過ごした）

よく使う！
☐ **have nothing to do with ～** ～と無関係である
⇔ **have something to do with ～** ～と何か関係がある

例文 I have nothing to do with the trouble.
（私はそのトラブルと無関係です）

間違えやすい！
☐ **have difficulty ～ ing** ～するのに苦労する
＊ have trouble ～ ing でも OK。difficulty の後に to 不定詞は置けないので注意。

例文 I had no difficulty finding the hotel.
（そのホテルはすぐに見つかった）

☐ **have an interest in ～** ～に興味を持つ
＊ have は take でも OK。

例文 I have an interest in statistics.
（私は統計学に興味を持っている）

☐ **have an eye for ～** ～を見る目 [鑑賞力] がある
☐ **have an ear for ～** ～を聞く耳 [鑑賞力] がある

例文 I have no ear for classical music.
（私にはクラシック音楽はさっぱりわかりません）

make + 名詞

makeの基本的な意味は「作る」ですが、名詞と結びついてさまざまな表現を作ります。

☐ make an impression on ～
～〈人〉に印象[感銘]を与える

例文 The film made a deep impression on me.
（その映画は私に深い印象を与えた）

☐ make a difference　差が出る；重要である

* make no difference は「差が出ない；どちらでもよい」。

例文 It will make a difference if he helps me.
（彼が私を手伝ってくれれば差が出るだろう）

よく使う!

☐ make a living　生計を立てる

* make は earn でも OK。

例文 She makes a living as a freelance writer.
（彼女はフリーライターとして生計を立てている）

間違えやすい!

☐ make friends (with ～)　（～と）仲良くなる

* friend は複数形にします。make a friend などと間違えないように注意。

例文 I made friends with my new classmates.
（私は新しいクラスメイトと仲良くなりました）

動詞+名詞の結びつき200

☐ **make a decision** 決心する

例文 Think it over before you make a decision.
（決心する前にそれをよく考えなさい）

☐ **make an excuse** 言い訳をする

例文 He is good at making excuses.
（彼は言い訳をするのがうまい）

☐ **make a complaint** クレームをつける

例文 Many people made complaints about the defective product.
（その欠陥品に多くの人々がクレームをつけた）

よく使う!

☐ **make an effort** 努力をする

例文 I'm making every effort to pass the certificate examination.
（私はその検定試験に合格するためにあらゆる努力をしています）

よく使う!

☐ **make a mistake** 間違える

例文 I made a few mistakes at the driving test.
（運転免許試験でいくつか間違えた）

☐ **make a noise** 音を立てる

例文 Don't make such a noise.
（そんな騒音を立ててはいけません）

☐ make it 間に合う

例文 I'm afraid we won't make it to our flight.
（私たちは飛行機に間に合いそうにない）

☐ make a presentation プレゼンテーションをする

例文 I made a presentation to our new client.
（私は新しい顧客にプレゼンテーションをした）

よく使う!
☐ make progress 進歩する

例文 He made remarkable progress in speaking English.
（彼の英会話は著しく進歩した）

よく使う!
☐ make sense 意味をなす

例文 This sentence doesn't make any sense.
（この文は意味をなさない）

よく使う!
☐ make a speech 演説をする

例文 I'm not used to making a speech in public.
（私は人前で演説をするのに慣れていない）

☐ make a promise 約束する

例文 I made a promise to lend him my car.
（私は彼に車を貸すことを約束した）

動詞＋名詞の結びつき200

よく使う！
☐ **make a reservation**　予約する

＊ reserve と同じ意味です。

例文 I forgot to make a reservation at the restaurant.
（レストランに予約するのを忘れた）

よく使う！
☐ **make money**　金をもうける

＊ make は earn でも OK。

例文 There is no easy way to make money.
（お金をもうける楽な方法はない）

よく使う！
☐ **make use of ～**　～を利用する

例文 They study how to make use of solar energy.
（彼らは太陽エネルギーを利用する方法を研究している）

☐ **make the most of ～**　～をできるだけ利用する

例文 Make the most of your opportunities to speak English.
（英語を話す機会をできるだけ利用しなさい）

☐ **make up one's mind (to do)**
　　　　　　　　　　　　（～する）決心をする

例文 I made up my mind to go to the U.S. to study.
（私は米国へ留学する決心をした）

take + 名詞

takeの基本的な意味は「取る；持って行く」ですが、makeやhaveと同様にさまざまな名詞と結びつきます。

よく使う！
☐ **take a break**　休憩する

＊ take は have でも OK。「休憩」は rest でも OK。

例文　Let's take a coffee break.
（休憩してコーヒーにしましょう）

例文　Let's take a rest in the shade of that tree.
（あの木陰で休憩しよう）

よく使う！
☐ **take a day off**　1日休みを取る

☐ **take a vacation**　休みを取る

＊「休み」は holiday でも OK。leave にも「休暇」という意味があります。take a sick leave（病気休暇を取る）のように使います。

例文　I was permitted to take three days off.
（私は3日の休みを取ることを許された）

☐ **take a shower**　シャワーを浴びる

＊ take は have でも OK。

例文　I was taking a shower when you called me.
（君が電話をくれたときにはシャワーを浴びていたんだ）

動詞＋名詞の結びつき200

間違えやすい！
☐ take medicine　薬を飲む
＊水薬でない限り、drink medicine とは言いません。

例文 Take this medicine after every meal.
（毎食後にこの薬を飲みなさい）

よく使う！
☐ take some measures　何らかの方策を取る
＊「方策」は steps でも OK。

例文 We should take some drastic measures.
（我々は抜本的な方策を取るべきだ）

よく使う！
☐ take care of ～　～の世話をする
＊同様の意味を look after でも表せます。

例文 Could you take care of the garden while I'm away?
（私の留守中に庭の世話をしてもらえますか）

☐ take charge of ～　～を担当する
＊「私はこのクラスの担任です」は I'm in charge of this class.。

例文 I'll take charge of this class for this year.
（私が今年このクラスを担当します）

☐ take the responsibility (for ～)
　　　　　　　　　　　　　　　（～の）責任を取る

例文 I'll take the responsibility for the trouble.
（私がそのトラブルの責任を取ります）

☐ take a nap　うたた寝する

例文　I took a nap after lunch.
（昼食の後でうたた寝をしました）

☐ take a chance　一か八かやってみる

例文　I took a chance and applied for the position.
（私は一か八かその職に応募してみた）

☐ take a deep breath　深呼吸する

例文　Take a deep breath and hold it.
（大きく息を吸って止めてください）

間違えやすい!
☐ take a taxi　タクシーを利用する

例文　Let's take a taxi in case we're late.
（遅れるといけないのでタクシーで行こう）

☐ take a note　メモを取る

例文　Take notes so you won't forget.
（忘れないようにメモを取りなさい）

☐ take one's time　ゆっくりやる

例文　Take your time. There is enough time left.
（ゆっくりやりなさい。時間は十分に残っています）

動詞+名詞の結びつき200

よく使う!
☐ take part (in ～) （～に）参加する
＊ take part は participate で言い換えられます。

例文 I'll take part in the speech contest.
（私は弁論大会に参加します）

☐ take a seat 座る

例文 Please take a seat and make yourself at home.
（着席してくつろいでください）

よく使う!
☐ take ～ 's place ～〈人〉の代理を務める

例文 Who will take the chairman's place?
（誰が議長の代理を務めますか）

☐ take advantage of ～
　　　　　　　　　～を利用する；～につけ込む

例文 The salesman tried to take advantage of my ignorance.
（そのセールスマンは私の無知を利用しようとした）

よく使う!
☐ take place 行われる
＊同様の意味を be held でも表せます。

例文 The conference took place in Osaka.
=The conference was held in Osaka.
（会議は大阪で行われた）

break + 名詞

breakの基本的な意味は「こわす；破る」です。

よく使う!

☐ **break a window**　窓ガラスを割る

＊同様に、「卵を割る」は break an egg (open) と言います。break a door open は「ドアを壊して開ける」です。
break には「壊れる」という意味もあります。break down は「故障する」で、「車が故障した」は My car broke down. と言います。過去分詞の broken は「壊れている」という意味の形容詞としても使い、「窓ガラスが割れている」は The window is broken. です。また、speak broken English は「片言の［ブロークンな］英語を話す」となります。

例文 **The teacher scolded him for breaking the window.**
（先生は窓ガラスを割ったことで彼をしかった）

☐ **break a rule [law]**　規則［法律］を破る
　⇔ keep a rule [law]　規則［法律］を守る

＊「守る」は observe、「破る」は violate も使えます。

例文 **Don't break the school rules.**
（校則を破ってはいけません）

☐ **break one's promise [word]**　約束を破る
　⇔ keep one's promise [word]　約束を守る

例文 **He broke his promise to return the money to me.**
（彼は私に金を返すという約束を破った）

動詞+名詞の結びつき200

☐ break the ice 〈場をなごませるために〉話の口火を切る

例文 The emcee made a joke to break the ice.
（司会者は話の口火を切るために冗談を言った）

よく使う!
☐ break one's leg 足を骨折する

＊「足首をねんざする」は sprain one's ankle と言います。「突き指する」は sprain one's finger です。

例文 I broke my leg while playing soccer.
（サッカーをしていて足を骨折した）

☐ break into laughter [tears] 突然笑い [泣き] 出す

例文 His funny gesture made us break into laughter.
（彼のこっけいな身振りを見て私たちはどっと笑った）

☐ break to pieces 粉々にこわれる

例文 The glass fell on the floor and broke to pieces.
（コップは床に落ちて粉々にこわれた）

☐ break up with one's girlfriend [boyfriend] 恋人と別れる

例文 I broke up with my boyfriend yesterday.
（きのう彼と別れたんです）

catch + 名詞

catchの基本的な意味は「つかまえる」です。

よく使う！

☐ **catch fish**　魚をつかまえる［釣る］

＊「魚を生け捕りにする」は catch a fish alive と言います。
＊「1匹の魚」は a fish ですが、「2匹の魚」も two fish と言います。two fishes ではないので注意しましょう。

例文 My son caught a big fish.
（息子が大きな魚をつかまえた［釣り上げた］）

よく使う！

☐ **catch a cold**　風邪をひく

☐ **catch the flu**　インフルエンザにかかる

＊ catch は get でも OK。「風邪をひいている」は have a cold。

例文 I caught a bad cold last week.
（先週ひどい風邪をひきました）

例文 I've caught your cold.
= You've given me your cold.
（君の風邪がうつったよ）

☐ **catch ～ 's attention**　～の注意を引きつける

＊ catch は draw でも OK。catch ～ 's eye（～の目を引く）という言い方もします。eyecatcher は「人目を引くもの；目玉商品」です。

例文 The demonstration caught the shoppers' attention.
（その実演は買い物客の注意を引いた）

動詞+名詞の結びつき200

☐ catch one's breath   息をのむ
＊ hold one's breath（息を止める）という表現もあります。

例文 We caught our breath at the stunt.
（私たちはその曲芸にかたずを飲んだ）

☐ catch sight of ～   ～を見つける（= find）
　　⇔ lose sight of ～   ～を見失う（= miss）
＊ I lost sight of the tour conductor in the crowd.
（私は人ごみの中でツアーコンダクターを見失った）のように使います。

例文 I caught sight of the top of the mountain.
（私たちに山の頂上が見えた）

☐ catch (on) fire   火がつく
＊「倉庫が燃えている」は The warehouse is on fire. で「倉庫に火をつける」は set [put] the warehouse on fire と言います。「たばこ［ろうそく］に火をつける」は light a cigarette [candle] です。

例文 The warehouse caught fire last night.
（昨夜物置が火事になった）

☐ get caught in a shower   にわか雨にあう
＊ get は be 動詞でもＯＫ。「にわか雨に捕らえられた」ということ。「にわか雨」を a traffic jam に置き換えれば「交通渋滞に巻き込まれた」という意味になります。

例文 I got caught in a shower on my way home.
（帰宅の途中でにわか雨にあった）

do + 名詞

doの基本的な意味は「する」ですが、特定の名詞と結びつくと「与える」という意味にもなります。

☐ do business (with ～) (～と) 取引をする

例文: We do business with several Chinese companies.
(当社は中国企業数社と取引しています)

よく使う!

☐ do one's best 最善を尽くす

例文: The important thing is (to) do your best.
(大切なことは最善を尽くすことだ)

☐ do one's duty 義務を果たす

例文: You must do your duty when you claim a right.
(権利を主張するなら義務を果たさねばならない)

よく使う!

☐ do the dishes 皿を洗う

＊do は特定の名詞と結びつき、「～を始末する」という意味になります。
- ☐ do the flowers (花を生ける)
- ☐ do the laundry (洗濯物を洗う)
- ☐ do the room (部屋の掃除をする)

例文: I've got to do the dishes.
(お皿を洗わなくちゃ)

動詞+名詞の結びつき200

よく使う！
☐ do the gardening　庭仕事をする

＊〈do + the +〜ing〉で「〜（の仕事）をする」という意味。
- ☐ do the cleaning（掃除をする）
- ☐ do the cooking（料理をする）
- ☐ do the shopping（買い物をする）
- ☐ do the washing（洗濯をする）

例文 I do the gardening every Sunday.
（毎週日曜日には庭の手入れをします）

☐ do 〜 good　〜に利益を与える；〜のためになる

＊good は「利益」という意味の名詞。日本語は「与える」ですが、ここでは give は使えません。

例文 Moderate exercise will do you good.
= Moderate exercise will do good to you.
（適度の運動は体によいでしょう）

間違えやすい！
☐ do 〜 harm　〜に害を与える

＊do 〜 damage でも OK。

例文 Smoking does you a lot of harm.
= Smoking does a lot of harm to you.
（喫煙はあなたの体に大いに有害だ）

間違えやすい！
☐ do 〜 a favor　〜に好意を与える；〜に親切にする

＊この形の do も「与える」の意味。favor の形容詞は favorable（好意的な）・favorite（お気に入りの）。

例文 Will you do me a favor?
= May I ask a favor of you?
（お願いがあるのですが）

draw + 名詞

drawの基本的な意味は「引く；線で描く」、drawerは「引き出し」です。
スポーツの引き分けも「ドロー（ゲーム）」と言いますね。

☐ draw a curtain　カーテンを引く

＊「ブラインドを（引き）上げる」は draw up [raise] the blinds です。

例文　Draw the curtains and open the window.
（カーテンを引いて窓を開けなさい）

よく使う！
☐ draw a line　線を引く

例文　Draw a line between public and private.
（公私の間に線を引きなさい）

☐ draw a lot　くじを引く

例文　Let's draw lots to decide who'll go.
（誰が行くか決めるためにくじを引こう）

☐ draw money (from a bank)
　　⇔ deposit money (in a bank)　（銀行から）お金を引き出す
　　　　　　　　　　　　　　　　　（銀行に）預金する

例文　I drew 100,000 yen from my bank account.
（銀行口座から10万円引き出した）

動詞＋名詞の結びつき200

☐ draw water　水をくむ

例文　Let's draw water before we start cooking.
（料理を始める前に水をくみに行こう）

☐ draw a conclusion　結論を引き出す

例文　What conclusion did the committee draw?
（委員会はどんな結論を引き出しましたか）

よく使う！
☐ draw a picture　絵を〈線で〉かく

＊draw は鉛筆やクレヨンなどで描く場合に使います。絵の具で描くときは paint a picture と言います。

例文　Can you draw a picture of a horse?
（馬の絵をかけますか）

間違えやすい！
☐ draw a map　地図をかく

＊「かく」ですが write は使いません。

例文　Will you draw me a map for your office?
（会社への地図をかいてもらえますか）

☐ draw up one's will　遺言状を作成する

＊draw up は「〈文書などを〉作成する」の意味。draw up a plan（計画を立てる）のようにも言います。

例文　I'll ask a lawyer to draw up my will.
（弁護士に頼んで遺言状を作ってもらいます）

get + 名詞

getの基本的な意味は「手に入れる」ですが、前置詞や副詞と結びつくとさまざまな意味になります。

よく使う！

☐ **get a chance** 機会を得る

例文 I got a chance to see a movie star.
（私は映画スターに会う機会を得た）

よく使う！

☐ **get a discount** 値引きしてもらう

例文 I got a 10 percent discount.
（10％値引きしてもらった）

よく使う！

☐ **get a job** 就職する

例文 He got a job through his family connections.
（彼は親戚のコネで就職した）

☐ **get a raise** 昇給する

例文 I want to get a (pay) raise.
（給料を上げてほしい）

☐ **get a refund** 払い戻してもらう

例文 I got a full refund on the ticket.
（切符を全額払い戻してもらった）

☐ get a tan　日焼けする

＊ get tanned も同じ意味です。

例文 You've got a deep tan.
（君はずいぶん日焼けしたね）

☐ get into shape　体調を整える

例文 I'm getting into shape for my trip.
（旅行のために体調を整えています）

間違えやすい！
☐ get to a station　駅に着く

＊前置詞の有無に注意！「そこ［ここ］に着く」は get there [here]、「家に着く」
　は get home です。

例文 I got to the station at 10:30.
= I arrived at the station at 10:30.
= I reached the station at 10:30.
（10時30分に駅に着きました）

☐ get rid of 〜　〜を取り除く（＝ remove）

例文 I can't get rid of this cold.
（この風邪がなかなか抜けない）

☐ get in contact with 〜　〜と連絡を取る

＊ get in touch with 〜でも OK。

例文 I haven't gotten in contact with him for a long time.
（私は長い間彼と連絡を取っていない）

give + 名詞

giveの基本的な意味は「与える」。しばしば後ろに「人＋物」の形を置きます。

よく使う！

☐ give (〜) an answer （〜に）返答をする

＊ give (〜) a reply でも OK。

例文 I sent him an e-mail, but he didn't give me an answer.
（私は彼にメールを送ったが、彼は返事をくれなかった）

☐ give 〜 a break 〜〈人〉を大目に見る

例文 For this once I'll give you a break.
（今回だけは君を大目に見よう）

☐ give a cry 叫ぶ

＊ give a shout でも OK。

例文 I gave a cry for help.
（私は助けを求めて叫んだ）

☐ give one's (best) regards to 〜
〜〈人〉によろしくと伝える

＊口語では say hello to 〜と言います。

例文 Please give my regards to your family.
（ご家族の皆さんによろしくお伝えください）

動詞+名詞の結びつき200

□ give ～ a discount ～〈人〉に値引きする
よく使う！

例文 Can you give me a discount on this camera?
（このカメラを私に値引きしてもらえますか）

□ give ～ a (helping) hand ～〈人〉を手伝う

例文 I gave my son a hand with his homework.
（私は息子の宿題を手伝った）

□ give (～) a smile （～に）ほほえむ

例文 She gave me a friendly smile.
（彼女は私に親しげにほほえんだ）

□ give ～ a ride ～〈人〉を車に乗せてあげる

例文 Shall I give you a ride to the station?
（駅まで車に乗せてあげましょうか）

□ give ～ a try ～をやってみる

例文 Come on! Just give it a try!
（だいじょうぶだ。やってみろよ）

□ give way (to ～) (～に)譲歩する

例文 I gave way to his persuasion.
（私は彼の説得に負けた）

go + 名詞

goの基本的な意味は「行く」です。

☐ go to work 仕事に行く

* go to school などと同様に、work には a や the はつきません。「オフィスに行く[通勤する]」は go to the office です。

例文 I go to work by subway.
(私は地下鉄で仕事に行きます)

よく使う!

☐ go on a trip 旅行に行く

* business trip なら「出張」。

例文 I went on a business trip to Hakata for three days.
(博多へ3日間出張しました)

☐ go to a barber (shop) 理髪店へ行く

例文 I go to the barber once every two months.
(私は2カ月に1回理髪店に行きます)

☐ go to Canada to study カナダへ留学する

* Canada の部分には国名・地名が入ります。国名を挙げずに「留学する」と言うときは go abroad to study。

例文 I'm going to the United States to study.
(私はアメリカへ留学するつもりです)

動詞+名詞の結びつき200

☐ go on sale　発売される

例文 The singer's latest album will go on sale next month.
（その歌手の最新アルバムは来月発売される）

☐ go out of one's control　〜の手におえなくなる

例文 The problem has gone out of our control.
（その問題は我々の手におえなくなった）

☐ go out with one's girlfriend [boyfriend]
　　　　　　　　　　　　　　　　恋人とデートする

＊「彼女をデートに誘う」は ask her out (on a date) と言います。

例文 I'm going out with my boyfriend on Saturday.
（土曜日は恋人とデートです）

☐ go Dutch　割り勘にする

例文 Shall we go Dutch?
= Shall we split the check [bill]?
（割り勘にしましょうか）

☐ go to the hospital　通院する

＊アメリカ英語では the をつけますが、イギリス英語では普通つけません。

例文 I go to the hospital once a week.
（私は週に1回通院しています）

keep + 名詞

「キープする」と日本語でも言うとおり、keepの基本的な意味は「保つ」です。

☐ **keep a diary**　日記をつける

＊「日記に書き込む」という動作は write in one's diary で表します。

例文　I kept a diary when I was a child.
（私は子どもの頃に日記をつけていた）

☐ **keep books**　帳簿をつける

例文　I learned how to keep books at the workshop.
（私は研修会で帳簿をつける方法を習った）

☐ **keep one's temper**　平静を保つ

⇔ lose one's temper　平静を失う；かっとなる

＊「平静」は head や cool でも OK。

例文　My boss usually keeps his temper.
（上司はたいてい平静を保っている）

☐ **keep a secret**　秘密を守る

⇔ leak a secret　秘密を漏らす

例文　I promised her to keep the secret.
（私は彼女にその秘密を守ると約束した）

動詞+名詞の結びつき200

☐ keep pace with ~　~に遅れずについて行く

例文　We have to keep pace with the times.
（我々は時代に遅れないようについて行かねばならない）

☐ keep an eye on ~　~を見張っておく（=watch）

例文　Please keep an eye on this baggage.
（この荷物を見張っておいてください）

☐ keep company with ~　~と親しくつき合う

例文　I've kept company with my neighbor for about 10 years.
（私は隣人と10年ほど親しくつき合っている）

☐ keep in touch (with ~)
　　　　　　　　　　　　（~と）連絡を取り合っておく

＊ keep in contact (with ~) でもOK。get in contact [touch](with ~) は「（~と）連絡を取る。」

例文　Let's keep in touch by e-mail.
（メールで連絡を取り合おう）

☐ keep ~ in mind　~を心に留めておく

＊ keep は bear でもOK。

例文　I'll keep your advice in mind.
（あなたの忠告を心に留めておきます）

lose + 名詞

loseの基本的な意味は「失う」です。

よく使う!

☐ **lose one's job**　失業する

＊次のようにも使います。
　☐ I lost my passport.（パスポートをなくした）
　☐ I lost my girlfriend.（失恋した）
　☐ I've lost my voice.（〈風邪で〉声が出ない）

例文 His company went bankrupt and he lost his job.
（会社が倒産して彼は失業した）

☐ **lose one's way**　道に迷う

＊ get lost も同様の意味。「私は道に迷っています」は I'm lost.。

例文 I lost my way, so I looked for a police station.
（私は道に迷ったので交番を探した）

よく使う!

☐ **lose weight**　やせる
　⇔ **gain [put on] weight**　太る

＊ I lost [gained] three kilograms.（3kg やせた［太った］）のようにも使います。

例文 The doctor advised him to lose weight.
（医者は彼に減量するよう忠告した）

動詞+名詞の結びつき200

> よく使う！

☐ lose a game　試合に負ける
⇔ **win a game**　試合に勝つ

例文：They lost the game by a score of 3 to 5.
（彼らは3対5で試合に負けた）

☐ lose face　面目を失う
⇔ **save face**　面目を保つ

例文：I lost face due to the failure.
（私はその失敗で面目がつぶれた）

☐ lose ground　劣勢になる
⇔ **gain ground**　優勢になる

例文：Our team is losing ground.
（我々のチームは劣勢になりつつある）

☐ lose one's confidence　自信をなくす

例文：I lost my confidence in my listening comprehension after the test.
（私はそのテストの後で自分の聞き取り力に自信をなくした）

☐ lose one's breath　息が切れる

例文：I sometimes lose my breath after walking to my office.
（会社まで歩いた後で息切れすることがある）

pay + 名詞

payの基本的な意味は「支払う」です。

よく使う!

☐ **pay the bill** 勘定を支払う

＊「勘定」は check でもOK。

例文 Let me pay the bill.
（私に勘定を支払わせてください）

☐ **pay a fine** 罰金を払う

例文 I paid a fine of 15,000 yen for speeding.
（スピード違反で1万5千円の罰金を払った）

☐ **pay 100 yen for ～** ～の代金として100円払う

＊ for は「～と引き換えに」の意味。「100」の部分には数字を入れます。

例文 I paid 20,000 yen for the camera.
＝ I bought the camera for 20,000 yen.
（私はそのカメラを2万円で買った）

☐ **pay off one's loan** ローンを完済する

例文 I have yet to pay off my housing loan.
（まだ住宅ローンを完済していません）

動詞＋名詞の結びつき200

☐ pay out of one's pocket　自腹を切る

例文 I paid out of my pocket.
（私は自腹を切った）

☐ pay through a bank　銀行振込で払う

例文 I'd like to have my salary paid through the bank (transfer).
（給料は銀行振込にしてください）

☐ pay in cash　現金で払う

＊「カードで払う」は pay with a credit card。前置詞の違いに注意しましょう。

例文 Will you pay in cash or by check?
（お支払いは現金と小切手のどちらになさいますか）

☐ pay in installments　分割払いをする

＊ installment は分割払いの１回分のこと。「一括払いをする」は make a lump-sum payment と言います。

例文 Can I pay in monthly installments?
（月賦で支払えますか）

☐ pay attention to ～　～に注意を払う

例文 Few people paid attention to the advertisement.
（その広告に注意を払った人はほとんどいなかった）

play + 名詞

playの基本的な意味は「遊ぶ；する」です。

よく使う！

☐ **play soccer**　サッカーをする

＊〈play + スポーツ名〉で「〜をする」という意味を表します。

例文　The boys like playing soccer.
（その男の子たちはサッカーをするのが好きだ）

間違えやすい！

☐ **play catch**　キャッチボールをする

＊play catch ball とは言いません。

例文　Let's play catch in the playground.
（運動場でキャッチボールをしよう）

よく使う！

☐ **play the piano**　ピアノをひく

＊〈play + the + 楽器名〉で「〜の楽器を演奏する」です。

例文　She is good at playing the piano.
（彼女はピアノをひくのが得意だ）

☐ **play a trick on 〜**　〜にいたずらをする；だます

＊1語で言うと cheat です。

例文　He likes playing tricks on his friends.
（彼は友だちにいたずらをするのが好きだ）

☐ play with blocks　積み木で遊ぶ

＊with は「〜を使って」という意味。次のようにも言います。
☐ play with toys（おもちゃで遊ぶ）
☐ play with sand（砂遊びをする）
☐ play with words（言葉遊びをする）

例文 The children are playing with (building) blocks.
（子供たちは積み木で遊んでいる）

よく使う！

☐ play a ... part [role]　…な役割を果たす

例文 She played a major part in the project.
（彼女はそのプロジェクトで主要な役割を果たした）

よく使う！

☐ play hide-and-seek　かくれんぼをする

＊play は「〜をして遊ぶ」という意味で、次のように使います。
☐ play house（ままごとをする）
☐ play doctor（お医者さんごっこをする）
☐ play tag（鬼ごっこをする）
☐ play beanbags（お手玉をする）
☐ play quoits（輪投げをする）
☐ play cards（トランプ遊びをする）
☐ play shogi（将棋をさす）
☐ play mah-jong（麻雀をする）
☐ play a video game（テレビゲームをする）

＊play には「〜のふりをする」という意味もあり、後ろに形容詞を置いて使います。
☐ I played sick.（私は仮病を使った）
☐ She's playing cute.（彼女はかわい子ぶっている）

例文 We used to play hide-and-seek at school.
（私たちはよく学校でかくれんぼをした）

put + 名詞

putの基本的な意味は「置く」です。

よく使う!

□ put ～ on the table ～をテーブルの上に置く

* put の後ろには場所を表すさまざまな言葉を置いて使います。
- □ put sugar in one's coffee（コーヒーに砂糖を入れる）
- □ put one's hat on one's head（頭に帽子をかぶる）
- □ put a pot over a fire（なべを火にかける）

例文 I remember putting the key on the table.
（カギをテーブルの上に置いたのは覚えています）

□ put ～ on the shelf ～を棚上げにする

* put は leave でも OK。

例文 The matter has been put on the shelf for three months.
（その件は3カ月間棚上げにされている）

□ put ～ on sale ～を発売する

例文 A new video game machine was put on sale today.
（新しいテレビゲーム機が今日発売された）

□ put ～ in order ～を整頓する

例文 We put the office in order twice a month.
（私たちは月に2回オフィスを整頓します）

動詞＋名詞の結びつき200

よく使う！

☐ put on one's clothes　服を着る
⇔ take off one's clothes　服を脱ぐ

＊ put on（着る；身につける）の反対は take off（脱ぐ；はずす）。put off（延期する）と混同しないように。I took off my coat.（私はコートを脱いだ）のように使います。また、服だけでなく、靴やかばん、めがねなどの場合にも使えます。
- ☐ put on one's shoes（靴をはく）
- ☐ take off one's glasses（めがねをはずす）

例文 I put on my clothes and went downstairs.
（私は服を着て下の階へ行った）

☐ put away (the) books　本を片づける

＊ away は副詞なので、後ろに置くこともできます。

例文 Put the books away in the bookcase.
（本を本棚に片づけなさい）

☐ put emphasis on ～　～を強調する

＊ 1語で言うと emphasize。また、put の代わりに lay や place も使えます。

例文 The lecturer put special emphasis on that point.
（講演者はその点を特に強調した）

☐ put off a game　試合を延期する

例文 We put off the game because of the rain.
（私たちは雨のために試合を延期した）

blow + 名詞

blowの基本的な意味は「吹く」です。

☐ blow a whistle　ホイッスルを鳴らす

例文　The umpire blew the whistle for halftime.
（審判はハーフタイムのホイッスルを鳴らした）

☐ blow bubbles　シャボン玉を吹く

例文　A girl is blowing (soap) bubbles.
（女の子がシャボン玉を吹いている）

☐ blow one's nose　鼻をかむ

例文　Blow your nose with this tissue.
（このティッシュで鼻をかみなさい）

☐ blow out a candle　ろうそくを吹き消す

例文　She blew out her birthday candles.
（彼女はバースデーケーキの上のろうそくを吹き消した）

☐ blow up a balloon　風船をふくらませる

例文　Let me blow up the balloon.
（ぼくが風船をふくらませるよ）

call + 名詞

callの基本的な意味は「呼ぶ；電話をかける」です。

よく使う！
☐ call a taxi　タクシーを呼ぶ

＊次のようにも言います
- ☐ call an ambulance（救急車を呼ぶ）
- ☐ call the police（警察に電話する）
- ☐ call in sick（病欠の電話をする）
- ☐ I'll call you later.（後で電話します）

例文　**Call** me **a taxi**, please.
（タクシーを呼んでください）

☐ call on a friend　友人を訪問する

＊visit（訪れる）と同じ意味です。He calls me ... だと「彼は私に電話をかけてくる」という意味になります。

例文　He **calls on me** once a week.
（彼は週に一度私を訪ねてくる）

☐ call off a game　試合を中止する

＊「コールドゲーム」はここからきた言い方です。call off は cancel（中止する）と同じ意味です。

例文　The **game** was **called off** because of the rain.
（試合は雨で中止された）

change + 名詞

changeの基本的な意味は「変わる；変える」です。

よく使う！

☐ **change one's mind** 心変わりする

例文 This is the last chance to change your mind.
（これが考えを変える最後のチャンスです）

よく使う！

☐ **change yen into dollars** 円をドルに交換する

＊ change は exchange でも OK。

例文 Where can I change (Japanese) yen into dollars?
（円をドルに交換できるところはどこですか）

☐ **change for the better** 好転する
　⇔ **change for the worse** 悪化する

例文 The situation is beginning to change for the better.
（状況は好転し始めている）

☐ **change jobs** 転職する

＊ change one's job とも言いますが、change job は間違い。change trains（列車を乗り換える）や change seats（席を替わる）などと同様の言い方です。

例文 I'm thinking about changing jobs.
（私は転職しようかと考えています）

hold + 名詞

holdの基本的な意味は「手に持つ；握る」です。

☐ hold the line 電話を切らずに待つ

例文 Hold the line, please. I'll get him.
（切らずにお待ちください。呼んでまいります）

☐ hold a stock 株を〈売らずに〉持っておく

例文 I'll hold the stock until it goes up by 10 percent.
（10％上がるまでその株を持っておくつもりです）

☐ hold one's tongue 黙る

例文 Hold your tongue!
（黙れ！）

☐ hold ～ under one's arm ～を腕にかかえる

例文 He is holding a parcel under his arm.
（彼は荷物を腕に抱えている）

☐ hold on to a rail 手すりにつかまる

例文 Hold on to the rail so you won't fall.
（倒れないように手すりにつかまりなさい）

leave + 名詞

leaveの基本的な意味は「去る；残す」です。

☐ leave one's umbrella (behind)　傘を置き忘れる

例文 I seem to have left my umbrella somewhere.
（どこかに傘を置き忘れたらしい）

☐ leave for America　アメリカへ向けて出発する

例文 I'm leaving (Tokyo) for America tomorrow.
（私は明日アメリカへ向けて（東京を）出発します）
※ leave from Tokyo ではなく leave Tokyo という点に注意。

☐ leave a matter to 〜　問題を〜に任せる

例文 I'll leave the matter to you.
（その問題は君に任せるよ）

☐ leave a lot to be desired　大いに改善の余地がある

＊ leave nothing to be desired なら「改善の余地は何もない；申し分ない出来だ」という意味になります。

例文 Your report leaves a lot to be desired.
（君の報告書には大いに改善の余地がある）

run + 名詞

runの基本的な意味は「走る」ですが、それ以外の意味でも使います。

☐ **run an ad** 広告を載せる

＊ run は put でも OK。

例文 They ran a want ad in the newspaper.
（彼らは新聞に求人広告を載せた）

☐ **run an errand** お使いに行く

＊ run は go on でも OK。

例文 Will you run a little errand for me?
（ちょっとお使いに行ってくれる？）

よく使う!

☐ **run a company** 会社を経営する

＊ run は manage でも OK。

例文 Mike hopes to run a company in the future.
（マイクは将来会社を経営したいと思っている）

よく使う!

☐ **run out of gas** ガソリンが切れる

＊「ガソリンが切れた」は We've run out of gas.。

例文 We're running out of gas.
（ガソリンが切れかけている）

see + 名詞

seeの基本的な意味は「見える;会う」です。I see.（わかりました）のように「理解する」の意味でも使います。

よく使う!

☐ see the sights of ～　～を見物する

＊「観光」は sightseeing、「観光地」は sightseeing [tourist] spot。

例文 Why don't we see the sights of the town?
（町を見物するのはどうですか）

よく使う!

☐ see a friend off　友人を見送る

＊「友人を駅へ迎えに行く」は meet a friend at the station。

例文 I'm going to see a friend off at the station.
（駅へ友人を見送りに行くところです）

間違えやすい!

☐ see a doctor　医者にみてもらう

＊ consult a doctor とも言います。meet a doctor とは言いません。

例文 You should see a doctor soon.
（すぐに医者にみてもらう方がいい）

☐ see little of ～　～にほとんど会わない

＊ see a lot of ～（～によく会う）、see nothing of ～（～に全く会わない）のようにも言います。

例文 I've seen little of her recently.
（最近彼女にはほとんど会いません）

set + 名詞

日本語でも「セットする」と言うように、setの基本的な意味は「置く；決める」です。

☐ set an alarm　目覚まし〈時計〉をセットする

例文　I forgot to set the alarm.
（目覚ましをセットするのを忘れた）

☐ set a date　日取りを決める

例文　We need to set the date and time for the meeting.
（会議の日時を決める必要がある）

☐ set up a company　会社を設立する

＊「設立する」は establish や found でも表せます。「創立記念日」は anniversary of (the) foundation です。

例文　When was your company set up?
（あなたの会社はいつ設立されましたか）

☐ set to work　仕事を始める

例文　It's about time you set to work.
（そろそろ仕事を始めてもいい頃だよ）

turn + 名詞

turnの基本的な意味は「回る；回す」です。

☐ turn a faucet 蛇口をひねる

＊turn は「ひっくり返す；裏返す」という意味でも使います。
- ☐ turn (down) a collar　えりを折り返す
- ☐ turn out an ashtray　灰皿を空にする
- ☐ turn (over) the pages　ページをめくる

例文 I turned the faucet, but no water came out.
（蛇口をひねったけれど、水が出なかった）

よく使う！

☐ turn (to the) right [left] 右［左］へ曲がる

例文 Turn right at the first corner.
（最初の角を右へ曲がりなさい）

☐ turn down an offer 申し出を断る

例文 Why did you turn down such a good job offer?
（なぜそんなにいい仕事のオファーを断ったの？）

☐ turn up the TV テレビの音を大きくする

＊もともとは「(スイッチをひねって)音量を上げる」の意味。「音を小さくする」は turn down です。

例文 Would you mind my turning up the TV?
（テレビの音を大きくしてもかまいませんか）

INDEX

0 degrees below zero — 33
0 degrees centigrade — 33
20-minute video — 77
4-exposure film — 97
0-minute walk — 106

A

carton of eggs — 75
fire broke out. — 83
mug of beer — 129
rainbow appeared. — 32
roll of film — 97
slice of bread — 16
train bound for ～ — 35
bandon a pet — 108
bdominal exercise — 103
cademic conference — 40
ccess the Internet — 52
dditional order — 50
djust a mirror — 24
dmission ticket — 94
dopt a plan — 44
dvance order — 50
dvanced class — 66
ffordable price — 70
fter-lunch coffee — 19
fter-sales service — 51
ir out a futon — 135
isle seat — 98
ll-you-can-eat restaurant — 129
musement park — 86
nalyze data — 55
nnual meeting — 41
nonymous call — 61
nswer a phone — 58
partment building — 114
pplication software — 57
rea code — 63
round-the-world tour — 96
rrange a conference — 40
rrange a party — 80
rrange a tour — 96
sk for a discount — 72

athletic sports — 100
attached file — 56
attend a class — 66
attend a meeting — 41
attend school — 64
automatic car — 89

B

bachelor party — 80
back a car up — 88
back street — 36
back tooth — 26
back up a file — 56
back up traffic — 38
bad weather — 28
bake bread — 16
balanced breakfast — 20
bar exam — 68
bargain price — 71
bath additive — 131
bath towel — 131
bay window — 115
be absent from school — 65
be expelled from school — 64
be good at driving — 90
be late for school — 65
be reflected in a mirror — 24
be suspended from school — 64
beach umbrella — 87
beat eggs — 17
beloved pet — 108
bicycle shed — 107
bitter coffee — 18
black coffee — 18
block a street — 36
block traffic — 38
blow a horn — 92
blow a whistle — 174
blow bubbles — 174
blow one's nose — 174
blow out a candle — 174
blow up a balloon — 174
board meeting — 41

boarding school — 65
boil water — 21/128
boiled egg — 17
boiling weather — 28
branch office — 48
break a rule — 150
break a window — 115/150
break an egg — 17
break into laughter — 151
break one's leg — 151
break one's promise — 150
break the ice — 151
break to pieces — 151
break up with one's girlfriend — 151
bring the laundry in — 120
browse the Internet — 52
brush one's hair — 22
brush one's teeth — 26
bubble bath — 131
budget meeting — 42
build a house — 112
bulky refuse — 122
bullet train — 35
bunk beds — 134
burnable garbage — 121
bus depot — 37
bus service — 37
bus stop — 37
business call — 61
busy street — 36
butter bread — 16

C

cable TV — 78
call a conference — 40
call a dog — 109
call a taxi — 175
call off a game — 175
call on a friend — 175
call the roll — 69
camping area — 82
camping equipment — 82
camping pot — 82

camping school 82	clouded mirror 24	decaffeinated coffee 19
cancel a class 66	club activity 69	decayed tooth 26
cancel a meeting 41	coeducational school 65	deep sleep 132
cancel a tour 96	coffee break 19	delete a file 56
cancel an order 50	coffee shop 19	deliver an order 50
canned coffee 19	cold front 32	department store 74
car pool 89	cold wave 32	design a house 112
car port 89	collect call 60	desktop computer 54
carry out a plan 44	collect garbage 121	develop film 97
carve meat 126	combat sports 100	dietary fiber 125
cash discount 72	commuter bus 37	dining table 127
catch ~'s attention 152	commuter ticket 94	direct train 35
catch a cold 152	company house 113	dirty laundry 120
catch a train 34	compress a file 56	discount shop 72
catch fire 82/153	computer literacy 54	discounted price 70
catch fish 152	computer screen 54	dish out the salad 128
catch one's breath 153	computer virus 54	distribute fliers 74
catch sight of ~ 153	concrete plan 44	disturb ~'s sleep 132
catch the flu 152	conference agenda 40	do ~ a favor 155
celebrate ~'s birthday 81	conference attendee 40	do ~ good 155
cell phone 58	conference room 40	do ~ harm 155
chain up a dog 109	confirm an order 50	do a push-up 104
chair a meeting 41	connect a computer to the Internet 52	do aerobics 105
change for the better 176	consult an oracle 84	do business 154
change jobs 176	continental breakfast 20	do exercise 103
change one's mind 176	conveyor-belt sushi bar 129	do one's best 154
change seats 98	copy a video 76	do one's duty 154
change trains 34	cost price 71	do one's hair 22
change yen into dollars 176	cost-effective plan 44	do one's homework 65
changeable weather 28	coupon ticket 94	do one's makeup 25
cheat on an exam 68	cram school 65	do sports 100
check data 55	crank call 61	do the cleaning 122
check for messages 62	creaking bed 134	do the dishes 154
checkout counter 74	cross a street 36	do the gardening 155
Chinese food 125	crowded train 35	do the laundry 120
cigarette butt 105	customer service 51	do the shopping 73
class reunion 66	cut a class 66	dog collar 111
clean a bath 130	cut a lawn 117	dog fight 111
clean fish 128	cut into a line 74	dog lover 111
clean up a room 118		dog paddle 111
cleaning equipment 122	dairy product 21	dog tag 111
cleanup duty 69	damage one's health 102	domestic car 89
clear the table 127	damp weather 28	door-to-door sales 46
clearance sale 46	day of the fair 86	double bed 134
close a street 36	dazzling light 133	download the software 57
close a window 115	dead-end street 36	draw a conclusion 157

INDEX

draw a curtain	156	
draw a line	156	
draw a lot	81/156	
draw a map	157	
draw a picture	157	
draw money	156	
draw up one's will	157	
draw water	157	
drinking buddy	129	
drinking party	80	
drive a car	88	
drive a friend home	90	
drive home	90	
drive to work	90	
driving rain	30	
drunk driving	90	
dry one's hair	22	
dry the laundry	120	
dump garbage	121	
dusty room	118	
duty-free shop	75	
dye one's hair	22	

E

early morning walk	106
ebb and flow	87
edit a file	56
educational software	57
elementary school	64
e-mail address	53
e-mail newsletter	53
emergency call	61
emergency conference	40
empty seat	98
empty street	36
enlarge a photo	99
entrance exam	68
entrance fee	86
erase a video	76
excessive exercise	103
excursion ticket	94
exercise a dog	109
express train	34
extend one's house	112
external call	60
extra service	51

F

face a mirror	24
face a street	36
fail an exam	68
faithful dog	110
false hair	23
false tooth	26
fancy-dress parade	86
farewell party	80
farm-fresh food	124
fasten one's seat belt	98
fast-forward a video	76
feather bed	134
feed a dog	109
fierce dog	110
fill up a car	88
fine rain	30
fire alarm	83
fire drill	83
fire engine	83
fire station	83
fireworks display	86
fix a tooth	26
fix breakfast	20
fix one's makeup	25
fix salad	128
fixed price	70
flexible plan	44
fluorescent light	133
flush a toilet	27
fly a kite	85
fold one's umbrella	31
fold the laundry	120
fold up a futon	135
folding bed	134
folding umbrella	31
food additive	125
food poisoning	125
forward an e-mail	53
fragrant coffee	19
free sample	75
freeze food	124
fresh bread	16
fried egg	17
fron desk	99
front seat	98

front tooth	26
front-row seats	98
fry vegetables	128
fuel-efficient car	89
full bath	131
full-length mirror	24
furnished apartment	114

G

garbage bag	121
garbage can	121
garbage truck	121
gargle with mouthwash	27
gas station	92
gather data	55
general meeting	41
get a bath ready	130
get a call	60
get a chance	158
get a discount	72/158
get a flat	92
get a job	158
get a majority vote	45
get a raise	158
get a refund	158
get a refund on one's ticket	94
get a seat	98
get a tan	159
get an idea	43
get caught in a shower	153
get in a car	88
get in contact with ~	159
get into shape	159
get off a train	34
get on a train	34
get perfect grades	69
get rid of ~	159
get to a station	159
gift certificate	74
give ~ a bath	130
give ~ a break	160
give ~ a call	60
give ~ a discount	72/161
give ~ a hand	161
give ~ a message	62
give ~ a ride	161
give ~ a try	161

185

give a cry … 160	greasy hair … 23	have no idea … 43
give a smile … 161	grill meat … 126	have nothing to do with ~ … 141
give an answer … 160	grind coffee … 18	have one's driver's license suspended … 92
give one's regards to ~ … 160	gross sales … 46	have one's hair cut … 22
give up a plan … 44	ground meat … 126	have one's way … 140
give way … 161	guard dog … 110	have second thoughts … 140
giveaway price … 71	guided tour … 96	have soup … 21
GM food … 125	**H**	head office … 48
go by train … 34	ham and eggs … 17	health club … 102
go camping … 82	hand mirror … 24	health examination … 102
go catch fireflies … 84	hand over a ticket … 94	health insurance … 102
go dig for clams … 84	hang out the laundry … 120	health spa … 102
go Dutch … 163	hang up a phone … 58	healthy food … 124
go fishing … 84	hard bed … 134	heat up food … 124
go for a drive … 90	hard exercise … 103	heated pool … 87
go for a jog … 105	haunted house … 86/113	heavy makeup … 25
go for a walk … 106	have ~ in common … 140	heavy rain … 30
go into business … 74	have ~ in mind … 140	heavy traffic … 38
go on a diet … 104	have a baby … 138	high school … 64
go on a hike … 84	have a class … 66	hit a car … 88
go on a picnic … 84	have a cold … 138	hit a jackpot … 81
go on a trip … 162	have a cup of coffee … 18	hit movie … 79
go on an errand … 74	have a dream … 139	hit on an idea … 43
go on sale … 46/163	have a fever … 139	hold ~ under one's arm … 177
go out of one's control … 163	have a good night's sleep … 140	hold a meeting … 41
go out with one's girlfriend … 163	have a good sleep … 132	hold a party … 80
go pick strawberries … 84	have a good time … 141	hold a stock … 177
go see cherry blossoms … 84	have a hangover … 129	hold on to a rail … 177
go shopping … 73	have a headache … 138	hold one's tongue … 177
go to a barber … 162	have a nightmare … 135	hold the line … 62/177
go to a movie … 78	have a sale … 46	homemade bread … 16
go to bed … 134	have a snowball fight … 84	host a party … 80
go to Canada to study … 162	have a strong grip … 105	hot bath … 130
go to school … 64	have a talk … 139	hot spa … 86
go to sleep … 132	have access to ~ … 140	house cleaning … 122
go to the dentist … 27	have an accident … 138	house for rent … 113
go to the hospital … 163	have an ear for ~ … 141	housebreak a dog … 109
go to the office … 48	have an effect on ~ … 139	housing loan … 113
go to work … 162	have an eye for ~ … 141	housing shortage … 113
good bargain … 75	have an interest in ~ … 141	hunting dog … 110
good idea … 43	have breakfast … 20	**I**
good service … 51	have crooked teeth … 26	illegal parking … 92
good weather … 28	have difficulty ~ ing … 141	imported food … 125
graduate from school … 64	have leftovers … 21	improve one's health … 102
graduate school … 65	have lunch … 139	impulse buying … 75
graduation ceremony … 69	have no appetite … 128	inbound train … 35

INDEX

incoming call … 60
increase sales … 46
individual sports … 100
indoor sports … 100
in-flight movie … 79
information office … 49
input data … 55
inspect a car … 88
install a phone … 58
install the software on a computer … 57
insurance against fire … 117
intermediate class … 66
intermittent rain … 30
internal call … 60
internet ad … 52
internet auction … 52
internet search … 52
internet site … 52
internet transaction … 52
internet user … 52
interpret a dream … 135
introductory class … 66
invalid ticket … 94
iron the laundry … 120
it began raining. … 30
it looks like rain. … 30
it stopped raining. … 30

J
join a tour … 96
join the end of a line … 74
jump rope … 85
junior high school … 64

K
keep ～ in mind … 165
keep a diary … 164
keep a pet … 108
keep a secret … 164
keep an eye on ～ … 165
keep books … 164
keep company with ～ … 165
keep in touch … 165
keep one's health … 102
keep one's temper … 164
keep pace with ～ … 165
keep the door locked … 116
keep up one's strength … 104

kill time … 81
knock on the door … 116

L
lack of exercise … 103
laptop computer … 54
late-night movie … 79
law office … 48
lean meat … 126
leash a dog … 109
leave a lot to be desired … 178
leave a matter to ～ … 178
leave a meeting … 41
leave a message … 62
leave a receiver off the hook … 62
leave a stain … 122
leave for America … 178
leave one's bed … 134
leave one's umbrella … 31/178
leave school … 64
leave the door open … 116
leave the lights on … 133
leave the office … 48
leave the TV on … 78
leave the water running … 122
let a bath drain out … 130
let a dog loose … 110
light breakfast … 20
light bulb … 133
light one's cigarette … 105
light sleep … 132
Lightning flashed. … 32
limited express train … 34
lively street … 36
load film … 97
local call … 60
local train … 34
lock one's bicycle … 107
lock the door … 116
long-distance bus … 37
long-distance call … 60
look for an apartment … 114
look in a mirror … 24
loose window … 115
lose a game … 167
lose a tooth … 26
lose face … 167

lose ground … 167
lose one's breath … 167
lose one's confidence … 167
lose one's job … 166
lose one's way … 166
lose weight … 104/166
lottery ticket … 95
low price … 70
lukewarm water … 122
lunch meeting … 42
lung power … 105

M
main street … 36
make a bed … 134
make a call … 60
make a complaint … 143
make a decision … 143
make a difference … 142
make a discount … 72
make a fire … 82
make a living … 142
make a mistake … 143
make a noise … 143
make a plan … 44
make a presentation … 144
make a promise … 144
make a reservation … 145
make a snowman … 84
make a speech … 144
make a toast … 128
make an effort … 143
make an excuse … 143
make an impression on ～ … 142
make coffee … 18
make friends … 142
make it … 144
make money … 145
make progress … 144
make room … 118
make sense … 144
make the most of ～ … 145
make up one's mind … 145
make use of ～ … 145
male dog … 110
marbled meat … 126
math class … 66

meal ticket	95
messy room	118
mid-term exam	68
mild coffee	18
mild detergent	122
mild winter	32
minimal makeup	25
miss a class	66
miss a train	34
miss breakfast	20
misty window	115
moderate exercise	103
moldy bread	16
mop the floor	119
move to a new apartment	114
movie director	79
movie star	79
movie theater	79
municipal office	48
muscular strength	105
My car skidded.	89
My cell phone doesn't work here.	63
my favorite sports	100

N

narrow street	36
national sports	100
nearest station	39
net price	70
new term	69
night fair	86
noon recess	69
notebook computer	54
nurse's office	49

O

observation deck	87
offer one's seat	98
office hours	49
office routine	49
office supplies	49
office worker	49
one's own house	112
one-way ticket	94
one-way traffic	38
on-line shopping	73
open one's umbrella	31
open the office	48

open-air bath	130
operate a computer	54
order sheet	50
organic vegetables	129
outbound train	35
outgoing call	60

P

package tour	96
pare an apple	128
park a bicycle	107
park a car	88
parking lot	92
part one's hair	22
pass an exam	68
passing lane	92
pat a dog	109
patrol car	89
pay 100 yen for ~	168
pay a fine	168
pay attention to ~	169
pay in cash	169
pay in installments	169
pay off one's loan	168
pay out of one's pocket	169
pay phone	58
pay the bill	168
pay through a bank	169
pedal a bicycle	107
perfect weather	28
permanent file	56
permanent tooth	26
permed hair	23
pet food	108
pet grooming studio	108
pet idea	43
pet loss grief	108
pet phrase	108
pet shop	108
phone book	59
phone booth	59
physical exercise	103
physical strength	105
pick up a phone	58
piled garbage	121
pirate video	77
pitch a tent	84

place an order	50
plant seeds	117
plastic bag	74
play a ... part	171
play a trick on ~	170
play a video	76
play cards	81
play catch	170
play hide-and-seek	171
play house	112
play soccer	170
play the piano	170
play with blocks	171
pleasant walk	106
plug in the video	76
polish the floor	119
popular sports	100
portable shrine	86
postpone a meeting	41
potluck party	80
pour coffee	18
pouring rain	30
practical idea	43
precipitation percentage	33
precooked food	125
prefectural office	48
premature plan	44
preserve food	124
press conference	40
price increase	71
price tag	71
price war	71
print film	97
print out data	55
process data	55
processed food	125
produce a movie	79
professional school	64
prohibit smoking	104
promotional video	77
public bath	130
public lavatory	27
public school	65
pull out a bad tooth	26
push a bicycle	107
put ~ in order	172

INDEX

out ～ on sale	46/172	
out ～ on the shelf	172	
out ～ on the table	172	
out ～ to bed	134	
out ～ to sleep	132	
put a futon in a closet	135	
put a proposal on the shelf	45	
put an idea into practice	43	
put away books	173	
put emphasis on ～	173	
put off a game	173	
put on one's clothes	173	
put out the fire	82	

Q

quote a price 70

R

raise a dog 109
raise the price 70
raw egg 17
raw meat 126
reach a sale of ～ 46
read ～'s palm 81
read ～'s fortune 81
read through a message 62
ready-built house 112
rearview mirror 92
reasonable price 70
receive an e-mail 53
receive an order 50
recently used file 56
reckless driving 90
record ～ on video 76
record a message 62
recover one's health 102
redecorate an apartment 114
redo one's makeup 25
reduce the price 70
refrain from smoking 104
register a house 112
regular meeting 41
release a movie 78
relocate the office 48
remodel a house 112
remove a stain 122
remove one's makeup 25
rename a file 56

renew an order 50
rent a bicycle 107
rent a video 76
rent an apartment 114
rental car 89
rental office 48
repair a car 88
repeat an order 50
reserve a seat 98
reserve a table 127
restart a computer 54
restrict traffic 38
retail price 71
return a call 60
revolving door 116
rewind a video 76
rich soup 21
ride a bicycle 107
ride a horse 85
roast meat 126
roll dice 85
roller coaster 86
room for improvement 10
round table 127
round-trip ticket 94
row a boat 85
run a bath 130
run a company 179
run a race 85
run an ad 179
run an errand 179
run out of gas 179

S

safe driving 90
sales campaign 47
sales figures 47
sales meeting 42
sales promotion 47
sales representative 47
sales tax 47
save a file 56
school building 65
school festival 65
school rules 65
school trip 65
school uniform 65

scrambled eggs 17
sea bathing 87
secondhand bookstore 75
secretary's office 48
see ～ on video 76
see a doctor 180
see a friend off 180
see little of ～ 180
see the sights of ～ 180
seeing-eye dog 110
self-opening umbrella 31
send an e-mail 53
send out the laundry 120
separate garbage 121
serve food 124
set a date 181
set an alarm 181
set fire to the wood 83
set one's hair 22
set the table 127
set to work 181
set up a company 181
shaggy dog 110
shampoo one's hair 22
share ～'s umbrella 31
share an apartment 114
share the table 127
shooting star 86
shoplift a book 74
shopping bag 73
shopping cart 73
shopping list 73
shopping mall 73
show a movie 78
show a ticket 94
shred cabbage 128
shut down a computer 54
shuttle bus 37
sister school 65
sit in a swing 85
six-mat room 118
skip a meeting 41
skip breakfast 20
slam the door 116
sleep on a futon 135
slice a loaf of bread 16

sliding door	116	
slow down	92	
slurp one's soup	21	
small apartment	114	
smoking area	104	
smoking car	104	
smorgasbord restaurant	129	
soft bread	16	
souvenir shop	86	
spacious apartment	114	
special discount	72	
special sale	46	
spectator sports	100	
speed trap	92	
spill one's coffee	18	
sports car	89	
sports day	101	
sports equipment	101	
sports event	101	
sports facility	101	
sports paper	101	
sports shoes	101	
spread out a futon	135	
square table	127	
staff discount	72	
staff meeting	42	
stale bread	16	
stand-up party	80	
staple food	124	
start up a car	88	
start up a computer	54	
station attendant	39	
stay in bed	134	
steam bath	131	
sticker price	70	
stiff hair	23	
stir one's coffee	18	
stop smoking	104	
storm warning	33	
straight hair	23	
stray dog	110	
strengthen one's muscles	105	
strict teacher	69	
strike a match	85	
strong coffee	18	
student council	69	
studio apartment	114	
subway station	39	
suggest a plan	44	
sultry weather	28	
summer resort	86	
surf the Internet	52	
sweep the floor	119	
swimming beach	87	
switch off one's cell phone	62	
T		
take ~ for a drive	90	
take ~'s place	149	
take a bath	130	
take a break	146	
take a chance	148	
take a day off	146	
take a deep breath	148	
take a drive	90	
take a message	62	
take a nap	148	
take a note	148	
take a photo	99	
take a seat	149	
take a shower	146	
take a taxi	148	
take a tour	96	
take a train	34	
take a vacation	146	
take a vote	45	
take a walk	106	
take advantage of ~	149	
take an exam	68	
take care of ~	147	
take care of a pet	108	
take charge of ~	147	
take medicine	147	
take one's pet for a walk	106	
take one's time	148	
take out garbage	121	
take part	149	
take place	149	
take shelter from the rain	30	
take some measures	147	
take the responsibility	147	
take up a sport	100	
talk in one's sleep	132	
taste the soup	128
teach a dog tricks	109
teacher's pet	108
telephone information service	59
telephone operator	59
telephone pole	59
telephone rate	59
tell ~ 's fortune	81
temporary file	56
tender meat	126
tentative plan	44
ten-thousand yen bill	74
terminal station	39
terrible weather	28
test a bath	130
The battery went dead.	63
The car crashed.	89
The car turned right.	89
The change is short.	75
the dimensions of a room	118
The dog is barking.	110
The dog is growling.	110
The dog is wagging its tail.	110
The film has jammed.	97
The fire died down.	83
The fire is smoldering.	83
The fire went out.	83
the first floor	119
the first train	35
The food has gone bad.	124
the heat of late summer	32
the last train	35
The light came on.	133
The light went out.	133
the look of the sky	33
The mirror broke.	24
The mirror cracked.	24
The mirror fogged.	24
The phone is ringing.	58
the rainy season	32
the rent for an apartment	114
The roof leaks.	117
the Sales Department	47
the second period class	66
The snow has melted away.	32
The stairs creak.	117

INDEX

The tree was struck by lightning. — 32
The weather will improve. — 29
The wind has died down. — 32
The wind is blowing hard. — 32
thin hair — 23
This food won't keep overnight. — 124
three-sided mirror — 24
three-story house — 113
Thunder rolled. — 32
ticket collector — 95
ticket gate — 95
ticket machine — 95
ticket office — 49/95
tidy a room — 118
tie a dog to a tree — 109
toast bread — 16
toll-free number — 63
tough meat — 126
tow a car — 88
traffic jam — 38
traffic offense — 38
traffic regulation — 38
traffic signal — 38
traffic ticket — 38
transfer a call — 60
transfer station — 39
travel agency — 99
treat ~ to dinner — 128
trim a hedge — 117
tropical day — 33
turn a faucet — 182
turn down an offer — 182
turn down the light — 133
turn off the light — 133
turn off the TV — 78
turn on the light — 133
turn on the TV — 78
turn over a bucket — 122
turn right — 182
turn the wheel — 92
turn up the TV — 182
TV personality — 78
TV set — 78

U

umbrella rib — 31
umbrella stand — 31

unanimous vote — 45
uncollected garbage — 121
unit price — 71
unlock the door — 116
unpleasant weather — 28
unplug the video — 76
unrealistic plan — 44
unsettled weather — 28
update a computer — 54
upgrade the software — 57
upper floor — 119
use a bathroom — 27
use a toothpick — 21

V

vacuum the floor — 119
vending machine — 74
video conference — 40
video game — 77
video phone — 58/77
video site — 77
visit a shrine — 84
vote for a proposal — 45

W

waiting list — 99
wake-up call — 61
walk a dog — 109
warm soup — 21
warm-up exercise — 103
wash rice — 128
washing machine — 122
watch TV — 78
water a garden — 117
water supply — 122
watermelon cracking — 87
wavy hair — 23
wax the floor — 119
weak coffee — 18
wear makeup — 25
wear one's hair long — 22
wear one's hair tied — 22
weather forecaster — 29
weather forecast — 29
weather map — 29
weather permitting — 29
weather station — 29
weed a lawn — 117

weekly meeting — 41
welcome party — 80
well-equipped office — 48
well-planned house — 112
wet laundry — 120
wet the bed — 134
white coffee — 18
window shopping — 73
winning ticket — 95
winter sleep — 132
wipe a window — 115
wipe the floor — 119
wipe the table — 127
wisdom tooth — 26
wooden house — 112
write down a message — 62
write over a file — 56
wrong number — 63
wrong station — 39

X

X-rated movie — 79

Y

year-end party — 80
yellow pages — 63
You're wanted on the phone. — 58

191

●著者紹介

佐藤　誠司 Seishi Sato

東京大学文学部英文科卒。広島県教育委員会事務局、私立中学・高校教諭などを経て、現在は㈲佐藤教育研究所を主宰。英語学習全般の著作活動を行っている。著書に『英作文のためのやさしい英文法』(岩波ジュニア新書)、『〈対訳つき〉シャーロック・ホームズの冒険』(PHP文庫)、『入試英文法マニュアル』(南雲堂)、『中学英語を5日間でやり直す本』(PHP文庫・共著)、『超整理！新TOEICテストビジュアル英単語』(ジャパンタイムズ・共著) など。広島県福山市在住。

カバーデザイン	滝デザイン事務所
本文デザイン／DTP	新藤 昇
本文イラスト	田中 斉
CDナレーション	Carolyn Miller
	横田 砂選

J新書⑱
魔法のコロケーション　英会話表現1000

平成23年（2011年）8月10日　初版第1刷発行

著　者	佐藤誠司
発行人	福田富与
発行所	**有限会社　Jリサーチ出版**
	〒166-0002　東京都杉並区高円寺北2-29-14-705
	電話 03(6808)8801㈹　FAX 03(5364)5310㈹
	編集部 03(6808)8806
	http://www.jresearch.co.jp/
印刷所	㈱シナノ パブリッシング プレス

ISBN978-4-86392-068-2　禁無断転載。なお、乱丁・落丁はお取り替えいたします。
© Seishi Sato 2011, All rights reserved.